THE
KINFOLK
ENTREPRENEUR

THE
KINFOLK
ENTREPRENEUR

IDEAS *for* MEANINGFUL WORK

NATHAN WILLIAMS

Ouur

NATHAN WILLIAMS
Editor in Chief

JOHN CLIFFORD BURNS
Editor

ANJA VERDUGO
Creative Director

ALEX HUNTING
Publication Designer

AMY WOODROFFE
Publishing Director

RACHEL HOLZMAN
Copy Editor

MOLLY MANDELL
Art Producer

SELECT CONTRIBUTORS:

CHRISTOPHER FERGUSON
Christopher has been capturing
fashion and landscape imagery for
the past 15 years. He has shot for *Vogue,*
Harper's Bazaar, Elle, Porter, and GQ and
published his own fashion magazine,
SUMMERWINTER Homme.

HARRIET FITCH LITTLE
Harriet is a British journalist and
editor. She writes about culture, people
and podcasts and has lived in Beirut,
Phnom Penh and London.

LASSE FLØDE
Lasse is a Norwegian photographer,
based in Oslo and Copenhagen. He
works with a variety of clients and
projects, including *The New York*
Times, Marie Claire, Bielke&Yang
and Snøhetta.

SARAH MOROZ
Sarah is a Franco-American journalist
and translator based in Paris. She
writes about cultural topics for *The*
New York Times, The Guardian, New York
magazine, *Artforum* and more.

SARAH ROWLAND
Sarah is a writer and editor who
has lived in Paris, London, Portland
and Nashville. Her work has been
published in *Monocle, Rolling Stone,*
Nylon, Esquire, The Guardian, Freunde
von Freunden and more.

DANILO SCARPATI
Danilo was born and raised in Naples,
Italy. His work has appeared in *T*
Magazine, 10 *Magazine, Vanity Fair* and
British Vogue and in various shows in
the USA and Europe.

MARSÝ HILD ÞÓRSDÓTTIR
Marsý is an Icelandic photographer
based in London. Her images are
influenced by her Nordic background,
her native contemporaries and the vast
untamed terrains she grew up in.

PIP USHER
Pip is a regular contributor to
Kinfolk and leading international
publications. After living in London,
New York and Beirut, she has made
Bangkok her home—for now. She
enjoys black coffee, eccentric people
and the works of Truman Capote.

ALEXANDER WOLFE
Alexander is a fashion, social and art
photographer exploring uncommon
scenes of everyday life in the Middle East.
His work has been published by *The New*
York Times, Vice, Brownbook and more.

For a full list of credits, see page 367.

Contents

PART THREE: CREATING A COMMUNITY

PART FOUR: TIPS

NATHAN WILLIAMS & DOUG BISCHOFF, COPENHAGEN

Introduction

We work to make a living. But living itself requires more than just income, and work (given how much time we spend doing it) can play a large part in how we define ourselves, our purpose in society and our quality of life.

During the 1970s, author Studs Terkel interviewed a diverse cross section of Americans for *Working*, a groundbreaking oral history in which he asked real people to "talk about what they do all day and how they feel about what they do."

He spoke to over 100 people—everyone from a cabdriver to a stockbroker, from a grave digger to a jazz musician. Their anecdotes led Terkel to conclude that work was ultimately "a search for daily meaning as well as daily bread, for recognition as well as cash, for astonishment rather than torpor; in short, for a sort of life rather than a Monday through Friday sort of dying." In the pages of this book, we meet people from around the world for whom work is more than a simple job to be discarded at the end of a long day. Some are enabled by the strength of a single vision, some through the power of partnership; and others' ideas serve to create and attract communities.

When we asked these business owners to speak frankly about their careers and values, certain words recurred: *grit*, *adventure*, even *naïveté*. We quickly discovered that becoming a successful entrepreneur extends beyond the strength of one's ideas and the ability to profit from them. It is dependent as much on private wounds as on public appearance; as much on the clients omitted from portfolios as on those mentioned in press releases; as much on the flash of brilliance as on the daily grind. We heard tales of widely respected industry leaders filing for bankruptcy to stay on top; of a designer dressing Michelle Obama from her home studio; of people serving as their company's CEO and also its janitor. Meaningful work, it seems, occurs during the process between an idea's conception and its realization.

Like Studs Terkel in his homage to jobs, we want work to improve the quality of life throughout the week: to help foster creativity, fortify relationships and forge new communities and to inspire people to make business more personal.

"Becoming a successful entrepreneur extends beyond the strength of one's ideas and the ability to profit from them."

Designed by Norm Architects, the Kinfolk
office in Copenhagen offers staff different
work environments, from an open-plan office
to private meeting rooms, a canteen and, right,
a private reading nook.

READER

EDUCATION

BIANCA CHANG
CRAIG OLDHAM
JACK SANDERS
JASPER MORRISON
JOCELYN GLEI
JOHN JAY
KENYA HARA

Ouur

1:

A Single Vision

Nobody goes it alone, but there are those who lead the way.

Nitzan Cohen

Nitzan Cohen's first venture into the world of design was thanks to a LEGO kit he received for his seventh birthday. "I grew up in a socialist, communal environment that only exists in Israel," he says of his childhood on a kibbutz. "The notion of design as a career wasn't something I was exposed to at all, so becoming a designer was a long process."

Nitzan had originally pursued a career in television, and tried to master sound and lighting in his teens. "I worked in an Israeli studio for a couple of years, but it became boring," he says. "I began playing around with props for fun, and that's when I realized that design is what excites and interests me."

Nitzan followed his dream, studying applied art at the Avni Institute of Art and Design in Tel Aviv and later attending the prestigious Design Academy Eindhoven in the Netherlands. After graduating, he interned with industrial designer Konstantin Grcic in Munich, Germany.

"I worked with Konstantin for five years—I learned so much. At the time, it was a very small studio. He's now one of the most significant designers worldwide," Nitzan says. "The cliché dream of every young design student is to open a studio, but for me the moment came when it just felt right to do my own thing."

He set out to establish his own multidisciplinary practice and opened Studio Nitzan Cohen in 2007. Nitzan's philosophies are rooted in the relationship between furniture design and the human body. "Furniture becomes part of people's everyday lives," he says. "It's about creating characters. One day, I'll hopefully find something of mine in a flea market! That's when I'll know that one of my pieces has actually lived."

As a designer, Nitzan combines research and conceptual design with his ability to translate visual language into objects and spaces. "I always have to question the question," he says of his business. "If you ask why and never settle for just because, then you have the power to crack problems. That's the moment when your design becomes full of promises and avenues open up."

Today, almost a decade since its founding, his studio works on projects that range from interiors and products to corporate consultancy and communication. "I think naïveté is one of the strongest motivators," he says. "I tell design students before they start their own studio to really, really think about it. Go to the mountains. Spend some time alone. If they come back completely sure that there's nothing else in the world that they would rather be doing, only then do I tell them to go for it."

"If you ask why and never settle for just because, you have the power to crack problems."

Opposite: Nitzan sits at his desk on a chair
of his own design. The chair, named He Said,
was produced as part of a project for Italian
furniture manufacturer Mattiazzi.

PROFESSION: BUSINESS NAME: LOCATION: ESTABLISHED:
GALLERIST   NILUFAR   MILAN, ITALY 1979

Nina Yashar

"All my friends thought I was crazy," says Nina Yashar as she reclines on a curved Ico Parisi couch that sits somewhat adrift in Nilufar Depot—the enormous furniture showroom she created in 2015. Nina is serene and charming as she discusses both how she came to expand her business from a store on Milan's luxurious Via della Spiga to this warehouse-style space and, above all, how she came to rule the roost when dealing furniture in this most taste-conscious of cities.

As one approaches the Depot in the industrial Derganino neighborhood, the air is sweet and distinctly alcoholic; next door is the Fernet-Branca distillery. What was originally devised as an architecturally enhanced warehouse to show off Nina's inventory has now become her prime show space. Regularly featured at Nilufar Depot are the works of Italian and international design masters such as Gio Ponti, Carlo Mollino and Arne Jacobsen—pieces that would be hard to find even in a design museum.

How does Nina define the Depot, which she took from concept to reality in just two years? "It's a small, living museum, where I select historical and contemporary pieces," she says. The word *small* hints at Nina's modesty; the 1,900-square-foot showroom feels vast and open. The word *museum* is perhaps more incisive. There are approximately 300 objects on display at any one time. "Somebody once counted 415 items, can you believe," she attests with the bemusement of someone unfamiliar with inventories. Nina sees herself as more curator-cum-gallerist than dealer. "Rotation is obviously subject to the selling and replacing of my objects," she says of editing the countless pieces on offer from her ever-changing stock. But she manages not to reveal anything of what makes such a complex task appear so seamless.

A small team of young men begins moving items between the display units that architect Massimiliano Locatelli masterfully constructed in the space. Nina is distracted and excuses herself politely from the interview. She dispenses some emphatic instructions without any of the finger-snapping or castigating tone one might expect in a world dominated by aesthetic

Opposite and right: At Nilufar, Nina displays pieces by masters like Carlo Mollino, Ettore Sottsass and Gio Ponti alongside more contemporary, cutting-edge designers that Nina has helped discover, such as Martino Gamper.

perfection. "I always tell these guys that they are artists too, that they should always try to do something creative," she says, returning.

For Nina, curation is innate, something that runs in her blood. It's also entwined with how she buys—a key aspect of her business. "I would say that 85 percent of my choices are not connected to my business plan," she says resolutely. "I've never bought anything just because I thought it would be easy to sell." At Nilufar, it's not so much that budgets are thrown out the window, it's more that they never existed to begin with. Nina's business strategy—based on gut feeling—yielded her little profit for a long time. But, she explains as she smokes a cigarette and seats herself back on the Parisi couch, "I want people to follow me. I don't want to follow them."

Nina was born in Tehran in 1957. Her family migrated from Iran to Milan, where her father set up a business selling Persian carpets. This heritage explains a lot about her mentality, she says. "I feel there's something genetic that allows me to make decisions. Sometimes I'm not really conscious of what I'm doing. If I were, I wouldn't take so many risks," she confesses wryly. Nina started her career by displaying some of the carpets from her father's stock. "My father always asked me: 'Why do you pick these strange, ugly things that very few people buy?'" When asked if perhaps her father unintentionally taught her what *not* to do, she laughs heartily and agrees. Her reflex, she explains, is to follow her passion.

Nina now provides furniture for Miuccia Prada (an old friend) and a whole raft of Milan and Europe's more moneyed clients. "If I hadn't focused on an elite market, I would have been bankrupt," she says with conviction. "My philosophy has always been to buy for only a few people." Nina's approach to business is based almost entirely on her own taste, which, luckily for her, presaged a global appreciation for classic contemporary design. What might appear to be a vague attitude to matters of business—a quintessentially artistic trait, perhaps—in fact hides a lucid, singular approach that identifies Nina as a true entrepreneur. "I think the aim of the dealer should be to show the client new things," she says with a smile, finally conceding to her profession.

Since 1979, Nina has managed to rack up an
inventory of over 3,000 collectible furnishings.
Her gallery, Nilufar Depot, is an essential
destination during Salone del Mobile, Milan's
annual furniture fair.

Ben Gorham

Ben Gorham's nose is big business. A former athlete, he made the improbable transition from professional basketball player to perfumer after founding Byredo in 2006. Despite a lack of formal industry training, Gorham has nimbly followed the smell of success, growing his cult fragrance brand into a global empire with a new store in Manhattan and a lucrative line of luxury goods.

"*Routine* is a terrible, terrible word for me because I'm on and off airplanes so much," he says. Gorham has just landed back in Sweden after a last-minute trip to New York, and he sounds tired. Travel is an integral element of his business, though—not only for practical reasons, but also because he collects new experiences along the way and jots them down in a notebook. Later, many of those scrawls end up as the Byredo fragrances that are neatly stocked on shelves around the world—fleeting thoughts that Gorham tries, quite literally, to bottle up.

Take the fragrance named Rose of No Man's Land, which was inspired by tales from the battlefields of World War I. Based on a story shared by his tattoo artist, it's a floral-scented tribute to the nurses who served on the front lines and rescued the wounded regardless of which side they fought on. In commemoration, many of the men tattooed an image of a nurse on their bodies once they returned home.

"I thought it was a beautiful story of a selfless act," Gorham says of the origin of the perfume, which has top notes of pink pepper and Turkish rose petals. "And I thought a fragrance would be a good way to tell the same story." It's a compelling insight into the process that transforms anecdotes drifting through Gorham's mind into the Byredo products sold at retailers that include Harrods, Colette and Barneys. But it's also a glimpse into Gorham himself—a man whose collection of tattoos (so numerous that he's "lost count") includes a nurse in a starched cap inked across his chest.

The brand's headquarters—formerly those of the Swedish postal service—provide further insight. An elaborate, dark green fireplace sits opposite generously proportioned windows that welcome in Sweden's scant sunlight. The ceilings are high; polished wooden wainscoting lines the walls. It's a potent symbol of Gorham's ascension from a boyhood spent on the outskirts of Stockholm (which he describes as "pretty poor, generally; lots of people in small apartments, lots of kids hanging out on the streets") to a life at the nucleus of his city's fashion and design scene. "The level of ambition, it's always been there," he says.

Byredo was born after a chance encounter with famed perfumer Pierre Wulff at a dinner party. "I met this guy and learned that smells, which I knew nothing about, were extremely powerful and could be used to evoke emotion in a very interesting way," Gorham says. Although he was

unemployed and living on a friend's sofa, Gorham traveled to Wulff's office in New York to ask for assistance. Next, he recruited renowned perfumers Olivia Giacobetti and Jérôme Epinette to translate his ideas into scents. "I feel fortunate that somebody believed in my ideas and was willing to finance them," he says without elaborating.

His very first fragrance, based on an essence of green beans that he remembers smelling on his father as a child, was deeply sentimental. Throughout its production, Gorham processed some of his own emotional history. "A lot of my work has fictional components, but it touches on bigger notions like love or loss or death," he says.

The grandeur of Byredo's headquarters could also, one suspects, serve as a visual testament to Gorham's dogged pursuit of the ultraluxe. While Byredo began as a perfume brand, the business is now a conduit through which Gorham can experiment with new interests. When he began to feel confined by the beauty framework, he turned his personal obsession with leather into a business. Now one of Byredo's camel-colored calfskin wallets retails for $500; handbags sell for thousands.

As Byredo mushrooms into a global brand, however, Gorham has come to accept that the business has a responsibility that reaches far beyond his own needs. "I realized that we're a commercial establishment that makes products for people," he explains. "I didn't engage in that thought for a very long time. I was self-indulgent—I was just making these products for myself. It was just me, me, me for a very long time. I started to realize that people were connecting with these products on an emotional level and that people were spending a lot of money. It made me feel some responsibility in my work, even though it's just perfume or just a bag."

Byredo, its name inspired by the old English word *redolence,* or agreeable fragrance, seems to mirror the sweetly scented life of Gorham. There's the rags-to-riches tale, the striking good looks and impeccable taste. If Gorham has demons, he manages them with the same iron will that has governed much of his life, first as an athlete and now as an entrepreneur. His success, he believes, comes from an "obsessive, nonstop, improving, evolving character that you have to possess."

Consumed by the intellectual challenges of leading a business, Gorham has recently returned to what he knows best: exercise. "I missed the physicality of the life I lived, so I've started running and lifting and boxing and wrestling and climbing and surfing and paddling and skiing," he says. "There's something quite meditative in that for me." With a wry note creeping into his voice, he adds, "I'm trying to figure out if it's some midlife crisis."

These days, his life has many facets to it: that of an entrepreneur, leader and family man. It's a sturdy foundation, one built to weather more than a newfound obsession with sports. As for his tattoos, he admits that the pain gets "worse every year"—although that hasn't stopped him.

That's the thing about Gorham: not much does. The tattoos continue to be inked, the business keeps growing, his ideas—so abundant that he jokes they're "part of [his] curse"—are corked and distributed around the world. "You have to believe in yourself," he says. "And then you have to realize that you'll probably get knocked down 10 or a hundred times. It's as much about getting up as it is about moving forward."

*"People were connecting with these products on an emotional level . . .
It made me feel some responsibility in my work."*

Ben was once a professional basketball player. "I made a decision to take all that energy and ambition and do something else," he says of his decision to change paths.

Sophie Hicks

Every morning, Sophie Hicks walks across the roof terrace that connects her home to her architecture firm. Despite living amid the abundance of restaurants and boutiques in London's Notting Hill neighborhood, Sophie remains steadfastly enclosed within, eating lunch at her desk and then swimming laps in her pool once the day ends. She is, says a colleague, "working while she's walking."

This relentless efficiency has allowed Sophie to pack a lot into the past four decades. First, there was her 10-year career in fashion, which included plum jobs as a fashion editor at *Tatler* and *British Vogue* in the '80s. She also acted in a Fellini film, worked as a stylist for her friend Azzedine Alaïa, earned a degree in architecture, had three children and launched her own business while still in the midst of her studies. "It's quite a lot," she says, a model of British understatement.

These days, Sophie has built a reputation as "fashion's architect." Her industry experience and eye for detail have made her a favorite for luxury brands that include Paul Smith, Yohji Yamamoto and Chloé (for whom, since 2002, Sophie has designed over 100 stores worldwide). Her work often melds a tough aesthetic to an unexpected sense of calm—including her own home, which she describes as looking "bare and unfinished" yet with a surprisingly homey feel.

"When fashion companies want their office designed, there's a huge gulf between the architect and the creative director. Architects are usually quite dry, and the fashion world is totally different," she says, dressed in a sharp collared shirt and glasses. Not only does Sophie successfully bridge this gap, but she also taps into her industry knowledge to create concepts for her clients.

While Sophie says she pays little attention to the work of her peers, she believes in the power of friendly competition to spur herself on. "When I swim on my own, I flounder up and down the pool," she says of her nightly ritual. "I'm quite lazy about it. When I'm swimming and someone else gets into the pool, I have quite a competitive streak. I swim more lengths, I swim faster and I get much better exercise."

For all its benefits, she's careful to keep this quality in check. "I think competitiveness is healthy when it's controlled and when you're not doing things purely for emotional reasons," she says. "It makes people raise their game, but you can't get out of hand. You have to not mind when you lose, which is very difficult sometimes. If you invest too much into your competitiveness, you lose perspective and it's a terrible crash when you don't succeed."

Sophie works from her home in London's
Notting Hill neighborhood. She has one
colleague, architect Tom Hopes, with
whom she has collaborated since 2011.

Ryo Kashiwazaki

Ryo Kashiwazaki is a young entrepreneur with an old-fashioned belief. As founder of Hender Scheme, a footwear and accessories brand best known for its coveted line of handcrafted leather sneakers, Ryo seeks to bridge the widening divide between Japan's traditional artisans and its new generation of talent. "It's not useful to compare who's superior or inferior," he says. "We need to exist together and share ideas."

Instead of cutting his teeth at an atelier, Ryo gained experience at a factory and a shoe repair shop. He prefers to think of himself as a maker rather than a designer. He started Hender Scheme in 2010, and for the first three years, he worked by himself. Hiring staff has expanded the brand's capabilities: Along with leather shoes, it now produces leather belts, jaunty nylon baseball caps and even a leather jacket that retails for more than $3,000. "There's a limit to what one person can do," Ryo says. Still, he prefers to run a tight ship that reflects the values at the core of his business; a small team of 13 takes care of all manufacturing, sales and PR. "We try to avoid outsourcing as much as possible, and we try to understand the products and the brand deeply," he explains.

At the heart of Ryo's business is an appreciation for the technical skills needed to craft a product that will have serious longevity. Take his Homage line, a range of sneakers that reimagines the classic silhouette of iconic sneakers in vegetable-tanned leather; a gleaming pair of box-fresh sneakers is replaced by the shine of well-worn cowhide. For Ryo, when a mass-produced mainstay of street culture is transformed into an artisanal object, its entire meaning changes. "The core idea of the brand is that we don't see our product as completed when it's displayed in stores," he says. "Only by actually being used by the customer do the products become closer to being finished."

In the early days of his business, Ryo was carried forward by youthful vim and vigor: "I had nothing to lose or to be worried about," he says. Growing more successful means that he's traded that initial—as he argues, necessary—naïveté for a more measured approach. Throughout, he has held true to his instincts. "I'm the one who makes decisions for my company, under all circumstances," he says. "Any advice is just advice—I regard it as opinion. If there are 10 people, there are 10 perspectives. You have to think carefully, be sensitive and make choices with your own will."

Above: Hender Scheme's atelier in the Asakusa
district of Tokyo — an area Ryo feels retains a
sense of *shitamachi*, or traditional culture.

Damir Doma

Damir Doma has always loved the Talking Heads track "This Must Be the Place." Only recently, however, have the lyrics taken on new significance. "Never for money, always for love," croons lead singer David Byrne—an idea that resonates with Damir so deeply that it gave name to a collection for his eponymous label. As he explains, in sentences as considered as the clothes he creates, "I would like to do things I love, and I want to do things I believe in."

Most creative entrepreneurs face a pivotal crossroads in which they must choose between commercial success and artistic freedom. This Croatian-born designer—whose rough, minimalist garments and androgynous silhouettes have gained him a cult following—has nimbly sidestepped such a dilemma. After cutting his teeth at the avant-garde ateliers of Antwerp-based designers Raf Simons and Dirk Schönberger, Damir launched his label in 2007 and quickly attracted a devoted following that includes Rihanna, Kanye West and rapper A$AP Rocky, who referenced Damir in his 2013 song "Fashion Killa." Since then, he has carefully cultivated the bread-and-butter of his business to support the more experimental creations that fulfill him as a designer: "There is a certain silhouette that stands for the brand, and that silhouette is the one that season by season gets picked up again and again," he notes. "This way, we can be free and innovative, and we don't have to be afraid," he says.

That desire for freedom has been instrumental throughout Damir's career, an itch—bolstered by the fearlessness of youth—that is responsible for the bold launch of his label when he was 25. If he had been a little older, perhaps more aware of the challenges ahead, he admits that pragmatism may easily have outweighed ambition. "I was very naive about it, or I would never have started," he confides. "It takes over your life. You have to give a lot, and you need to be aware of that."

A decade later, dewy-eyed enthusiasm has been replaced by the reality of running a growing business, which relocated from Paris to Milan in 2015 to be closer to its suppliers. ("Most things that happen in fashion

Damir also collaborates with other brands. Pictured opposite is a pair of Siru sunglasses that were produced for German eyewear brand Mykita.

happen for much more pragmatic reasons than people pretend," Damir notes wryly.) Now at the helm of a team of more than 30 people, Damir has been forced to pick up practical knowledge to support his design skills. The pressure to provide not just for himself but also for all of his employees is sometimes crippling; he cannot, as he points out, simply move to Australia on a whim. The weight of responsibility is balanced by exhilarating creative freedom.

"In the last 10 years, I've never had a feeling that I have to go to work," he says. "I'm in quite an amazing position—I can go to the office, and there are people there who help me create what I have in my mind. When I see it that way, it's fantastic."

Most of the brand's early struggles—scant finances, an abundance of chaos, plus the frenetic dictates of an industry in which labels are expected to churn out 10 collections a year—have been ironed out as it has matured into a sustainable business. Over the past decade, Damir and his team have worked hard to streamline the brand's output. Now there are four collections a year, and the one show per season includes both menswear and womenswear. "Everything is very much planned and controlled," he says.

Like his role model, Giorgio Armani, Damir has maintained complete autonomy over his label, yet there are no plans to build an empire. Instead, Damir intends to stay small, selective and true to his ideals. "I don't feel the way I felt five or six years ago, when it was all about capital growth—to grow from 10 million into 20 million into a 40 million turnover. There was no limit," he says. "Today, I would be happier to have a stable business with a good profit that means I can invest in projects that I like."

Which leads him back to the Talking Heads. A thirst for money will only lead so far—it's love that carries you through. "It's important to believe in something," says Damir. "If you don't, you are not able to go the extra mile. And if you have your own business, you need to go the extra mile all the time."

DAMIR DOMA

Damir named his Spring/Summer '17 show
after his favorite mantra, "Never for money,
always for love."

FORMS AND SYMBOLS

This Paris flat belonging to the gallery owner Yves Lambert doesn't betray its previous incarnation as a workshop. Andrée Putman, who converted it and could – had she wished – have turned it into an open plan loft, has chosen instead to make it into a conventional apartment with clearly demarcated rooms. Now the walls are strictly white and the ordinary wooden parquet floors have been painted in a dark shade of grey. So far, nothing exceptional. But then, disorientation creeps in. The apartment's main furniture pieces – the sofa in the living room and the ottoman in the room – have had their functions put in doubt. They've been transformed into fleeting, ghostly presences with cloth coverings conjure up visions of mediumistic ectoplasm. For reassurance one has to cling to the plain columns, fresh off some set, standing around like film extras with a lightweight nonchalance that – paradoxically – makes you realise they have their feet planted very firmly on the ground.

Azéde Jean-Pierre

"It's not a brand unless you create desire. People must want to buy into it," says Azéde Jean-Pierre. Based in New York, Azéde founded her independent ready-to-wear fashion label in 2012. Shortly afterward, she was hailed as "the next big thing" in the competitive world of fashion.

Her ability to walk a fine line between fashion and art, femininity and edge, allows her to achieve her goal of designing clothing that will be cherished by her clientele; her brand has become a favorite of influential women including Michelle Obama and Solange Knowles. But long before she started creating dresses for others, she was busy designing her own. The first thing she made was her own prom gown at the age of 16.

Azéde studied fashion at Savannah College of Art and Design and went on to work with Ohne Titel and Ralph Rucci before pursuing the launch of her label. She has always focused on creating apparel that empowers its wearer. "My brand is a reflection of the women that inspire it, and they come from multicultural backgrounds," she says. "They're world-traveling explorers driven by passion." Through her designs, she celebrates and highlights what's naturally feminine, showcases the strength of a free spirit and pushes the boundaries of functionality and innovation. "Growing up in a family of five daughters gave me a broader understanding of women, and that informs my design aesthetic. I've learned that perspective and personality are two things that greatly influence style."

A native of Pestel, Haiti, Azéde is influenced by her cultural background and her upbringing in Atlanta. "I'm the middle child of immigrant parents—the daughter of conservative working-class people," she says. "I learned quickly to be persistent, perceptive, to trust my instincts and think openly but hold on to my values."

Her output is a reflection of and a bridge between these cultures: For example, with her Spring/Summer '16 collection, she started working with artisans in developing countries to manufacture specific elements for each garment. Long-term, her goal is for her company to help reduce poverty and promote sustainable growth in developing countries.

Azéde is driven by a passion for individual expression. She aims always to reflect other women's identities through her designs, while staying true to herself as she steers her business. "A person who is innovative in their thinking," she says, defining what the word *entrepreneur* means to her. "It's about making up rules and trusting your intuition enough to take major risks based on it."

In 2016, Azéde was selected for *Forbes* 30 Under 30—an annual list of the brightest young entrepreneurs, innovators and game changers.

In 2014, Azéde cold-emailed the White
House and presented herself. It worked:
Michelle Obama commissioned her to design
a dress that she wore on the cover of
Essence magazine.

Azéde arrived in the United States as a
refugee, via a camp at Guantanamo Bay,
Cuba. At her first presentation at Paris Fashion
Week in 2016, Azéde's collection took
inspiration from French Creole—the language
of Haiti, her motherland.

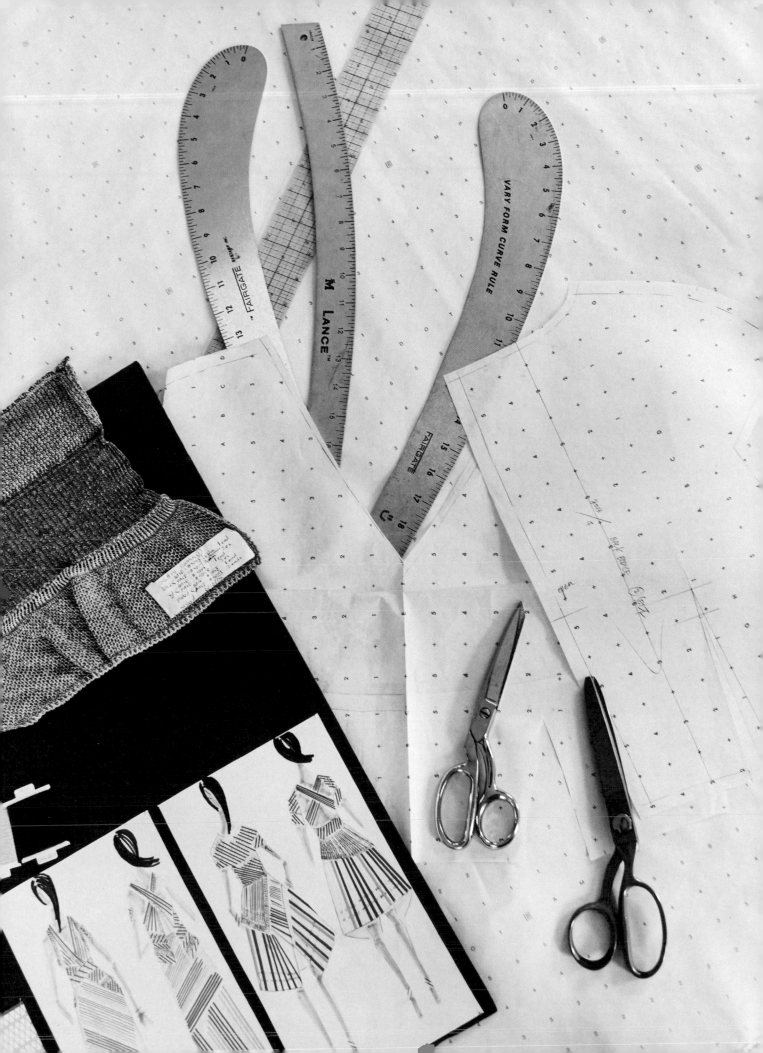

Kevin Ma

How does Kevin Ma spend his free time? Whichever way the question is asked, an answer is not forthcoming. "To be honest, I get so bored," he says politely, almost apologetically. There are no crack-of-dawn workouts, no carefully planned family getaways or binge-watching weekends. Social media offers few clues because Kevin rarely uses his personal accounts. His style is crisp but low maintenance—plain tees or button-down shirts—and while he still likes to collect sneakers (there are boxes of them cluttering his otherwise utilitarian office), he doesn't do so obsessively. "It's just a pair of shoes," he points out. "It only gives you temporary satisfaction. After that high fades, you're on to the next."

This might seem like sacrilege coming from the man who turned his sneaker blog into a digital media and retail company when it filed for initial public offering on the Hong Kong stock exchange in April 2016. But Kevin's strategy was always premised on the recognition that fashion changes, and fast. It's there in the name: When Hypebeast was created in 2005, "hype beast" was a slang label ascribed to people obsessed with chasing new trends. Now the term is synonymous with the empire built by Kevin. Over the last 12 years, Hypebeast has expanded to cover all aspects of popular culture and gradually added new verticals to its portfolio, including a creative studio, an online store and a print magazine. In early 2017, the company nabbed a spot on *Fast Company*'s annual list of the world's 50 most innovative companies, its editors praising Kevin for "uniting sneakerheads into a lucrative demographic."

Kevin's success story is a tale made for a digital age. Born in Hong Kong in 1982, he set up Hypebeast using Blogger shortly after graduating from the University of British Columbia because he felt forums and Japanese magazines didn't cover the whole spectrum of sneaker news. For six months, Kevin juggled his passion project with a job in finance. When the income generated by the blog (initially via platforms like Google AdSense) topped his salary, he quit to focus on Hypebeast full-time.

In the early days, Kevin worked alone and around the clock, rarely leaving the house (he didn't own a laptop). He didn't read business books or seek out mentors: "I really kept my head down. I did not ask people for help. I did not ask people for advice," he says. Was it exhausting? "I was

super-passionate and really into it, so it didn't bother me." Incidentally, this is why Kevin finds it so hard to answer questions about his free time: He fills every available moment with work.

Kevin moved Hypebeast into its first office in 2009 when the company had 10 employees. This was the messiest phase of expansion, he says, because he had no experience of managing people. A self-described introvert, he thinks he made mistakes with early hires because the pool of people he knew was small. When the lease on the office was up, Kevin decided that there was little point to Hypebeast having a physical space other than that it facilitated Ping-Pong matches. For a year, everyone worked from home: "That way I didn't have to dress, I didn't have to commute. It just saved a lot of time."

Without the benefit of pre-existing connections or a passion for networking, how did Kevin fashion Hypebeast into the sort of influential brand that counts Lupe Fiasco and Kanye West as vocal fans? "I don't want to say people just came to us . . . but they did just come to us," he says, modest but direct. "I guess it was good timing."

Of course, progress happens less haphazardly now. Kevin moved Hypebeast back into offices in 2011 and chose Hong Kong for the company's global headquarters because of its strategic placement; it's a transit hub for international brands and allows him to keep abreast of streetwear culture and trends in nearby Japan. He has built a team of 124 people who complement his talents, and says that learning to deploy the abilities of others is a skill that entrepreneurs could benefit from learning earlier in their careers than he did: "You've got to learn to let go and trust the people around you. You've got to let them do the work because if you don't, your company is not going to grow."

If he were graduating now, what would he do? This is the only question that gives Kevin real pause. "I think it's in my personality to want to do something different. That 'entrepreneur spirit,' I think I have it a little," he says. Where exactly that spirit might lead him in today's landscape, he is less certain. Kevin is keenly aware that timing had a big part to play in his blog's meteoric rise, which came before digital media hit saturation levels. "I don't think I could do Hypebeast. It's just over. That phase is over," he says.

But he has no qualms about the company's future, despite the increased competition. What would happen to Hypebeast if sneakers suddenly went out of fashion? For Kevin, it's an amusing but inconsequential thought, and one that has never troubled him. Over the course of a decade, he has put down roots that cover too much ground to be so easily extracted. "We started off with sneakers, and we're proud of that, but we've evolved," he says. "If sneakers went out of fashion, we'd just talk about different stuff."

Alongside its original online endeavor, Hypebeast has diversified into a print magazine and an online store, selling the very products that it promotes. Its website continues to attract 3 million unique visitors per month.

MOODBOARD

Captivating, hypnotic movement
to convey kinetic energy and
athletic moments against subtle,
muted tones to demonstrate **con**
effortless style.

OARD

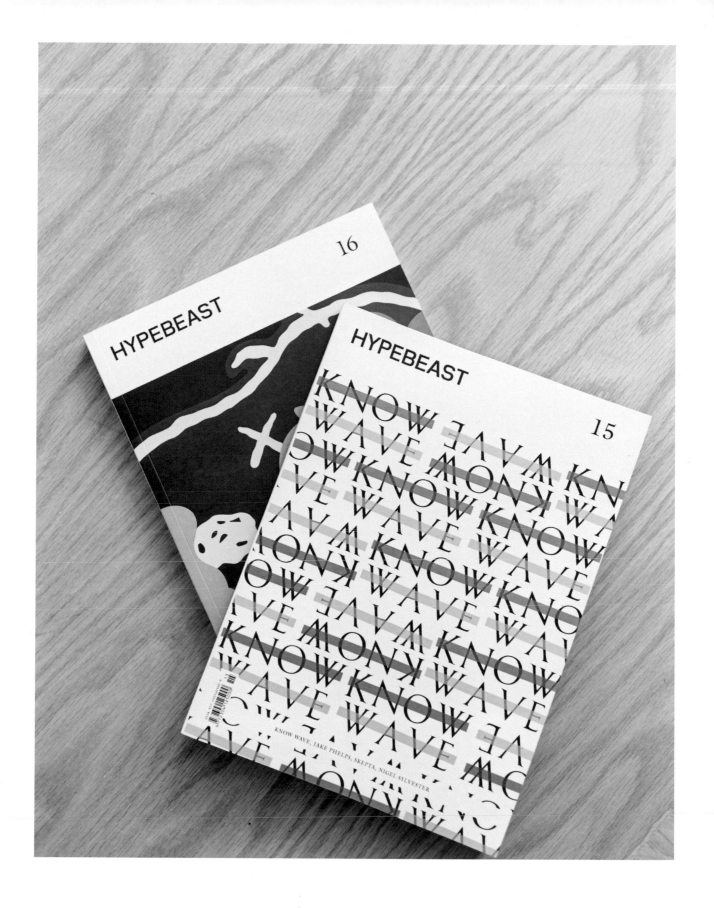

Each issue of *Hypebeast* magazine addresses a
certain theme. Issue 15, pictured above, is titled
The Foundation Issue.

PROFESSION:
GRAPHIC DESIGNER

BUSINESS NAME:
DESIGN ARMY

LOCATION:
WASHINGTON, DC, USA

ESTABLISHED:
2003

Pum Lefebure

"Good design should please the eyes and activate the mind," says Pum Lefebure, chief creative office of Design Army. "It hits an emotional chord. It's not only about aesthetics," she says. For Pum, there are no rules within the world of design: "You have to follow your heart," she says.

Design Army is a testament to her ability to combine love and work. In 2003, she and her husband, Jake, founded the company in Washington, DC. Together, they've become leaders in corporate identity, conceptual design and distinctive art direction. As the company's driving force, Pum leads Design Army to dream up high-profile campaigns for an impressive roster of clients including Ritz-Carlton, Bloomingdale's and the Academy Awards. "I believe we're in charge of our destiny, so I believe in taking risks," she says.

Pum's passion for design and curiosity about the world guides the development of her projects and empowers her team. Growing up in Bangkok influenced her aesthetic sensibilities. "The overdose of culture in Thailand made me focus on smaller things," she says. "Everything is distinctive—dances, art, food, color palettes—but I learned to drown out the noise and focus on fine details." In Thailand, Pum had been trained to draw from a young age. "We were given photographs and told to copy them," she says. "But one day, I became sick of copying. That's the moment I decided to break free," she says.

Today, she prides herself on bringing a global sensitivity to every project, based on her wide range of cultural experiences. She allows her intuition to guide her decision-making, and her balance of artistic and strategic thinking has proven that good design is the cornerstone of a good business. "Our process is old-school. I present an idea to the team, and then I make them all go dream," she says. "I'm constantly pushing them to create something new—something they didn't even know they were capable of creating."

Pum believes it's necessary to design an emotional experience to be successful. "Do you believe in love at first sight?" she asks. "The first visual is the ultimate seducer—it flirts and mesmerizes. It triggers feelings that create something more than a fleeting encounter." And to her, this is only the beginning: After the initial visual jolt comes the breadth and depth of a fully rounded experience.

"Successful entrepreneurs have to have the ability to dream big. When you dream, you do so alone. It comes from somewhere inside—from your gut, from your past or maybe from your experiences," she says. "You have to create a vision of exactly what you want. Of course you don't know how the hell you're going to get there, but you dream. You figure it out."

One of Pum's handbooks for how to succeed is advertising expert Paul Arden's *It's Not How Good You Are, It's How Good You Want to Be.*

Pum says that the best piece of business advice
she has received is to know her creative worth.
"Do not undercharge, or undersell," she says.
"All clients like expensive regardless of whether
they can afford it or not."

13

Merci !

GROW
YOUR OWN
MUSH-
ROOMS

Interiors Atelier AM

Armando Cabral

"I don't think you have to be an Ivy League graduate, just a risk-taker," says Armando Cabral as he considers his leap from international model to creator of an eponymous men's footwear label. But as his daily 5 a.m. wake-up will attest, the path to successful entrepreneurship still asks much of those who take it. "It requires a lot of persistence, perseverance and hard work," he concedes.

Born in the West African country of Guinea-Bissau and raised in Portugal, Armando was first taken to a runway class when he was 17. (Good looks run in the family: His brother, Fernando, is also a well-known face on the modeling circuit.) By 2006, Armando had hit the big time, strutting the catwalks for Louis Vuitton, Dior Homme and Thierry Mugler. Each interaction with a major brand was a new opportunity to study the industry up close, providing pearls of business wisdom that he stored away for later use. "I was always attentive and keen to learn about the business," he remembers.

Eventually, the glitz and glamour of fashion shows wore thin. Armando—who studied business in London before his modeling career took off—briefly toyed with finance during an eight-month stint at a small, private wealth management firm. "Five months in, I realized it wasn't for me," he admits. "Soon after, modeling picked up again and I decided to earn the capital necessary to start the Armando Cabral brand."

In 2008, he founded a premium footwear line. The shoes—from red deerskin leather high-tops to the shaggy rabbit fur "Jetset" slipper—were designed with Armando's own lifestyle in mind, prioritizing sleek design, comfort and Italian craftsmanship. "The Armando Cabral man is a global nomad," he says. "I believe the modern man requires a shoe that conveys a timeless aesthetic without sacrificing comfort." To this day, he adheres to the simple advice of J. Crew CEO and personal mentor Mickey Drexler, who once told him to always listen to his customers. As a result, his shoes walk a fine line between aspirational and affordable. "I wanted to create something that was beautiful and comfortable but was not needlessly expensive," he explains.

Now his brand is sold at Mr Porter and Bloomingdale's, with a flagship store in Lisbon. "To me, being an entrepreneur is a gift," Armando says. "My greatest professional accomplishment has to be building this brand. It's something I've done from the ground up, on my own. I can't imagine doing anything else."

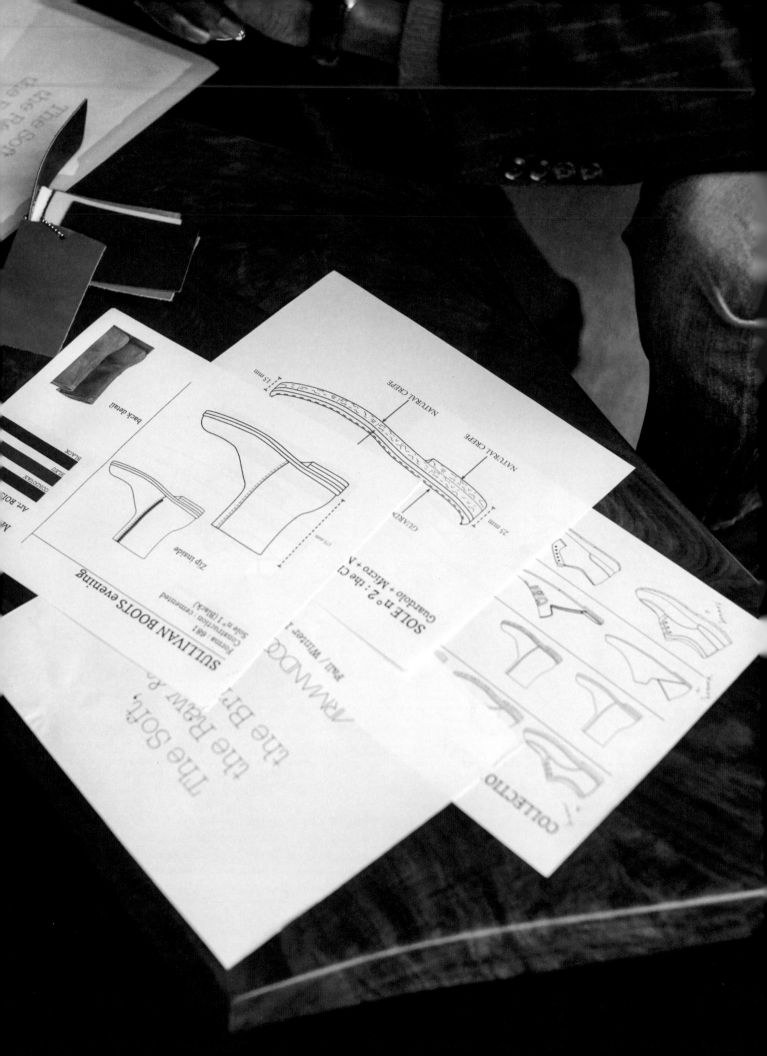

Armando says that designing shoes has been
his lifelong dream. "I use minimalist silhouettes
that are juxtaposed to complex interior
constructions," he says of his designs.

Armando cites Andrew Rosen, CEO of Theory, as a role model: "His attention to detail and quality and his minimalist philosophy have always informed my own attitude toward business."

PROFESSION:
CONFECTIONER

BUSINESS NAME:
SWEET SABA

LOCATION:
NEW YORK, USA

ESTABLISHED:
2015

Maayan Zilberman

"I live in this funny little sugarcoated world," confesses Maayan Zilberman from her studio in New York's Chelsea neighborhood. The artist-cum-confectioner, sporting a patterned purple sweater, cat-eye glasses and a bright pop of pink lipstick, has translated this sunny outlook into sugary creations. Sweet Saba, the business she launched in late 2015, crafts brightly colored, nostalgia-influenced candy that speaks to Maayan's vivid imagination. "I make things that make people want to break out their phones and show people," she says of her vintage-inspired candy cassette tapes, sunglasses-shaped lollipops and gleaming evil-eye sweets.

After graduating from the School of Visual Arts with a degree in sculpture, Maayan turned her attention to women's undergarments thanks to a chance conversation with some business school graduates looking to launch a lingerie label. She was soon appointed creative director, despite being clueless as to how bras were stitched together. But always up for a challenge, she headed straight to Macy's, bought some lingerie and promptly took the pieces apart. "I wasn't so interested in fashion per se. I was interested in the challenge of making something," Maayan recalls.

In 2007, she launched The Lake and Stars, her own lingerie label, cheekily named after a Victorian euphemism for a woman skilled in the bedroom. The collections' clean lines and strong interpretations of femininity quickly won followers, but Maayan and her business partner reached a crossroads after five years. Though their designs were stocked in all the right places, growing pressure to expand exposed them to the realities of how scaling up could affect their creative involvement. "Everyone told us that we needed to back further and further away from the design process—to touch things less and less with our hands," Maayan says. It wasn't what she wanted, but the eventual decision to close The Lake and Stars gave her space to explore new forms of expression. "It's so important as an artist and as an entrepreneur to be able to shift gears and think in a different language," she says. "That's how you keep growing and keep servicing your customers. You have to refresh over and over."

For Maayan, that came in the guise of cane sugar. Already a dab hand in the kitchen, with a side business baking elaborate cakes for select clients, she began to search for another creative medium with a longer shelf life. "I've always loved candy, and I knew that sugar could take on real sculptural qualities as the crystals transform," she says. Crafting homemade goodies started as a fun hobby, but Maayan quickly amassed an online following once she began regularly posting photographs of her colorful creations to Instagram. Soon, orders were flooding in—aided, in part, by her existing connections in the fashion and art worlds. When she finally sat down to do the math, she realized that her sugar habit had the potential for considerable success.

"I'm way happier than I was before because I'm doing things that put smiles on people's faces. It's affordable for most people, and you don't have to go to Barneys to find it," she says. Her sweets range from $12 for a bracelet to $30 for a long-stem candy rose and upward for her bespoke candy artworks—which, Maayan confirms, her clients most certainly do not eat.

Alongside Sweet Saba, Maayan has had a number of other projects. There was Radar, a line of mood rings that began when Maayan sought to replace her favorite piece of jewelry—a mood ring purchased in a toy store that had started to turn her finger a grubby shade of black. After pricing it out, she realized it would be far more cost-effective to produce 500 rings and peddle the rest at a profit. Her hunch paid off; Maayan made all of her money back and more. "I have friends who have tons of ideas, who are so creative and are some of the best artists I know," she reflects. "But I feel like what makes me an entrepreneur is that I come up with the idea, then I make it. And then I figure out how I can make it for many other people, and create an industry out of it, and employ other people."

Then there is her line of marijuana edibles, scheduled to launch toward the end of 2018. "It's a no-brainer," she says of her plan to enter the fastest-growing industry in the United States. Maayan expects the products to appeal to an aesthetically driven clientele seeking marijuana as a means of relaxation or as an alternative to prescription drugs. "I'm looking to create something geared toward people who would shop at Whole Foods," she says. "People who want to know what they're putting into their body and who want something that doesn't look like it came from a rave."

Maayan's world is kooky, colorful and fervently fun. Her fittingly sweet disposition is supported by a knack for transforming offbeat ideas into commercial ventures; she looks to Martha Stewart's one-woman empire as proof that sweetness and success go hand in hand. "I got to meet her and was featured in her magazine," she says. "I respect someone who maintains a veneer while being tough and getting what they want."

Maayan was born on a kibbutz in northern Israel before her family immigrated to Canada. Sweet Saba is named in honor of her grandfather, whom she would assist in the kitchen as a child. *Saba* is Hebrew for "grandfather."

"I respect someone who maintains a veneer while being tough and getting what they want."

In 2016, Maayan created a line of
confectionery exclusively for the Whitney
Museum of American Art and staged a candy
installation at Art Basel Miami Beach.

2:

The Power of Partnership

Through confluence or conflict, doubling up makes for a singular business.

Britt Moran & Emiliano Salci

In an industry distracted by "just-so" austerity and asceticism, Dimore Studio designers Britt Moran (opposite, left) and Emiliano Salci are waving a flag for indulgence. "We try to push our clients as much as possible with colors, materials and furniture from different eras," says Britt.

Since the Milan-based business was founded in 2003, Dimore Studio has designed interiors for some of the world's chicest brands, counting fashion houses Fendi and Boglioli, restaurateur Thierry Costes and hotelier Ian Schrager as clients. "'Dimore' in Italian means dwellings, but it conjures up images of old villas clinging to their aristocratic origins," says Britt, adding that "a nostalgia surrounds the name."

The duo's anomalous approach to design—which melds historical influences with a contemporary interpretation—starts when Emiliano and Britt settle upon a fantasy figure to guide each project's narrative. In 2015, in Guadalajara—a city in western Mexico famed for its tequila and mariachi music—they transformed a 1940s colonial mansion into the retro-inspired, defiantly colorful Casa Fayette hotel. Throughout, they imagined Luso-Brazilian samba singer Carmen Miranda "arriving at the hotel with trunks of clothes, singing late into the night on the patio and having breakfast by the pool the next day late in the afternoon."

Emiliano, a vision of European excess in extravagant prints and wild socks, is the designated "crazy genius," while Britt—clad in more neutral clothing—"has to be there to make sure the client thinks we're going to move through the projects." Their yin and yang personalities are underpinned by a shared sense of industriousness. "We're very, very hands-on, and I think that's one thing the client expects from us," says Britt. "To have certain projects look the way you want, you have to be very diligent and

Dimore Studio's magpie-like tendencies
bring eclectic design pieces together.
Opposite, a floor lamp by Hans Bergström
for Ateljé Lyktan sits next to two armchairs
by Marco Zanuso for Arflex and a vintage
Italian coffee table.

meticulous." The pair's shared vision stretches beyond the parameters of a traditional business partnership. They have lived together "forever," says Britt, making them housemates too. A demanding workload, coupled with the industry's numerous social engagements, means that they spend most waking moments together. Despite the intimacy, their relationship remains platonic.

"I know—it's a strange arrangement," Britt says. "I do think that to get everything done, that's how it has to be. We start talking about everything in the morning, we have lunch together, we have dinner together."

"Our life is centered on what we do," adds Emiliano. "We work 24/7 because we enjoy what we do so much. It seems natural to work at the office and to take work home."

As in any close relationship, there are dramatic blowups, particularly when the two are faced with demanding deadlines. For Emiliano and Britt, the trick is to clear the air. "We have a great group of people that we work with and it's kind of like a family. And, as in every family, there's usually a good shouting session, then we all kiss and make up and go have a drink together," says Britt. Such intimacy provides a comforting constancy as their acclaim grows. "I'm really happy to have someone to bounce ideas off," he admits. "It would be a very daunting position to be just the one person."

Together, Emiliano and Britt now have their own line of fabrics and a furniture design company alongside their regular client projects and participation in international fairs.

Emiliano and Britt start each of their projects by creating a fictional person to guide the narrative. Then, they create a mood board to help visualize an imaginary world.

119

"It's kind of like a family. There's usually a good shouting session, then we all kiss and make up and go have a drink together."

Opposite: Sofas and armchairs from Dimore
Studio's own furniture collection are paired
with pieces by Gio Ponti and Ico Parisi.

Woo Youngmi
& Katie Chung

"I wanted Korean men to dress more stylishly and elegantly," says Woo Youngmi (opposite, right) as she remembers the genesis of her menswear label, Solid Homme, in 1988. Just short of three decades later, what started as Youngmi's desire to make over her fellow citizens is now a global empire: Her two lines, Solid Homme and the more upscale Wooyoungmi, are now stocked by retailers throughout Europe, the Middle East and North America.

Today, Youngmi answers to the name "Madame Woo." Clad in a dark overcoat with her hair cropped into a neat pixie cut, she sits comfortably at the forefront of South Korean fashion. But she remembers growing up in an inward-looking and conservative society—still recovering in the brutal aftermath of the Korean War—when design was dismissed as an unnecessary extravagance.

"I was lucky to grow up with parents who had an artistic perspective," she says of her architect father and piano-teacher mother. Imported fashion magazines and art books allowed Youngmi glimpses of a wider world; even her family home looked more creative than its neighbors. "The house my father built was a unique pentagon shape, whereas most houses had the same simple box structure during that period in Korea," she says. "I can remember flowers in a beautiful vase on a vintage wooden table, and my father wearing a bathrobe and reading the newspaper with his cigarette."

In 1978, Youngmi enrolled at Seoul's Sungkyunkwan University to study fashion; five years later, she represented South Korea at a fashion competition in Osaka, Japan, and won. A brief dalliance with womenswear design confirmed her suspicions: She didn't like it. "The clothes I had to design were limited in style and they had to conform to an antiquated image of women," she says. "I realized that my taste wasn't particularly feminine. I was more comfortable with the restrained detail of menswear design."

Solid Homme launched in 1988, the same year that South Korea hosted the Olympic Games. Its pioneering aesthetic—well-cut, contemporary and influenced by European design—resonated with Seoul's surge of newly wealthy Korean men. Within a year, the business was debt-free; in the decade that followed, the label was picked up by the country's leading department stores and became one of the nation's most beloved menswear brands. "Solid Homme rode the wave of huge economic expansion," Youngmi says of her brand's skyward momentum during those formative years.

As her home country gained economic traction on the world stage, Youngmi's ambitions also grew global. "I wanted to design for more men, outside of South Korea, and be tested by the European market," she says. With a different demographic in mind, she launched a second label, Wooyoungmi, at Paris Fashion Week in 2002. "Wooyoungmi expresses my vision of a more creative man," explains Youngmi. "It emphasizes exceptional quality and precise and innovative tailoring, and takes its European influences one step further thanks to our design studio in Paris."

For its Fall/Winter '17 collection, Youngmi channeled Victorian playwright and devoted aesthete Oscar Wilde. Extravagantly ruffled collared shirts, oversized coats and slate-gray velvet trousers cultivated an air of slouchy sophistication that expanded the brand's repertoire beyond its natural tendency toward minimalism. In part, this evolution can be traced to the arrival of Youngmi's daughter, Katie Chung, as the brand's co-creative director. "Katie brought a breath of fresh air into both brands," says Youngmi. "We share an understanding of each brand's DNA that ensures that the Wooyoungmi man remains but, viewed from Katie's perspective, gains a new attitude."

Fearless and forever adapting, Youngmi is enduringly relevant. Her labels have not only brought personal success over the decades, but have also proved instrumental in South Korea's emergence from nascent fashion scene to internationally admired barometer of style. "I felt no limits in myself as a woman designing menswear," she says of that first gutsy decision to launch her business all those years ago. Her advice to budding entrepreneurs is simple: "Pursue authenticity, focus on your core values and work with persistence."

Below: Before Katie (right) was announced as co-creative director with her mother, she had been the brand's art director and had produced its advertising campaigns, often in collaboration with artists.

Opposite: At the label's flagship stores in Paris and Seoul, Wooyoungmi also stocks a selection of other branded products, including stationery, tools, accessories and barware.

When picturing the man for whom she designs,
Youngmi once told *The New York Times* that her
muse was Kang Dong Won, the South Korean
actor. She has since convinced Won to walk her
shows in Paris.

Following a successful collaboration with online retailer Mr Porter in 2014, Youngmi was named by *The Business of Fashion* as one of the 500 people shaping global fashion the same year.

PROFESSION:
PUBLISHERS

BUSINESS NAME:
BROWNBOOK

LOCATION:
DUBAI, UAE

ESTABLISHED:
2006

Rashid & Ahmed Bin Shabib

Rashid Bin Shabib (opposite, left) is seated behind his desk at the offices of *Brownbook*, the bimonthly, Dubai-based periodical he launched with his twin brother, Ahmed. Wearing a *kandoura*, tousled dark curls bidding an escape from his white *thobe*, Rashid cuts a dashing figure. He's internationally educated and erudite, as comfortable in Emirati national dress as he is in slim-cut trousers and owl-shaped glasses. He looks around him and sees the Middle East and North Africa as a region rich in tradition and beauty. And yet, whenever he flicks on the news, it's the same old story. Death. Destruction. Dark, heavy stuff. It's hard not to let it wear him down.

"You read it, and then see it reinforced and reappropriated. It becomes an echo chamber to some extent," he says of the mainstream media's myopic portrayal of the Middle East. "We're always hearing about topics of religion, tolerance, different value sets. That's important, without a doubt. But that agenda is not our fight. Our job here is to show the progressive and optimistic side of the region."

Cue *Brownbook*, the brothers' decade-old magazine that comes out of a desire to showcase a side of the Middle East that other media outlets largely ignore. Born and raised in the United Arab Emirates, the pair credit their grandfather—a businessman who later became Minister of Transport and Infrastructure—with instilling in them an academic interest in the evolving role of cities and society. Their mother, who raised them alone, was another powerful role model ("She's very liberal, open-minded, progressive," says Rashid). This conflation of interests and values can be seen on the thick pages of *Brownbook*, which describes itself as an urban guide to the Middle East and North Africa and profiles a sprawling cast of characters from Lebanese aristocrats to Jordanian weathermen.

The brothers launched *Brownbook* in 2006—a bold move considering that many established magazines were disintegrating into financial disarray. But their decision was driven by practicalities; as Rashid explains, a magazine was the most useful vehicle for their ambitious storytelling. "Magazines are still the most progressive medium in which you can compile and build a narrative about a specific topic," he says. "I think the only reason we still exist is because we treat it as a utility." (*continued*)

Even when dealing with divisive topics like Palestine—the mere mention of which sends people into the political trenches—the Bin Shabibs are careful to remain neutral. They see the confrontational tactics employed in other countries as counterproductive in light of the more subtle social codes of their region. The brothers believe that *Brownbook*'s success lies in its intuitive approach to such etiquette, their focus on resolutely optimistic stories encouraging readers to look at what's working in other countries in the region as an impetus for progress in their own. "Instead of saying, 'All of this is wrong,' we rephrase it as, 'Here's what's going right,'" Rashid adds.

Alongside *Brownbook*, the brothers explore what they term "cultural engineering" in its many guises—through publishing, exhibitions and, most notably, urban development projects. Their fascination with the importance of civic spaces led to the duo's first architectural undertaking around the same time that *Brownbook* launched. They settled on repurposing an old nail factory in Al Quoz, a largely industrial area of Dubai that *The New York Times* once deemed "the gritty opposite of glamorous." A warehouse space was transformed into a co-working campus called Shelter, with local entrepreneurs and freelancers enticed to its desks by no rent, a relaxed, open-plan layout and regular networking events. The idea was to bring small business owners together. On a deeper level, though, it was a bid to forge community.

"I'm far more interested in how we can create spaces for people to come together, whether that's formed in a physical place or a nonphysical one—as in being a member of a regional collective," says Ahmed. He points to their recent work at Al Khazzan Cadillac Park, an inner-city green space, in which they launched a free public library with content curated by *Brownbook*. Again, the aim was to foster meaningful interaction and, Ahmed hopes, to encourage these exchanges to take place outside of Dubai's ubiquitous shopping malls. "It brings people together to meet around productive social experiences," he says. "It allows people to meet, create workshops, set up markets and so forth without the need to just consume."

Open-mindedness and *hopefulness*: These are words perhaps not usually applied to the Middle East. But then again, Western media tends not to look in the right places. In their battle to balance progress with tradition, Rashid and Ahmed document their region's complexity without looking to provide easy answers. They know there are none. "*Brownbook* and our other projects try to reinforce our identity to the world because that's what the rest of the world does—constantly reiterates its identity," Rashid says. "And then it serves to reaffirm our identity within ourselves."

Rashid and Ahmed both consider themselves urbanists and employ an in-house architect to work on built projects around Dubai. Their first project, Shelter, was nominated for an Aga Khan Award for Architecture in 2010.

"Instead of saying, 'All of this is wrong,' we rephrase it as, 'Here's what's going right.'"

Brownbook began as a print supplement to Brown Bag, a now defunct online retail venture that the Bin Shabib twins started.

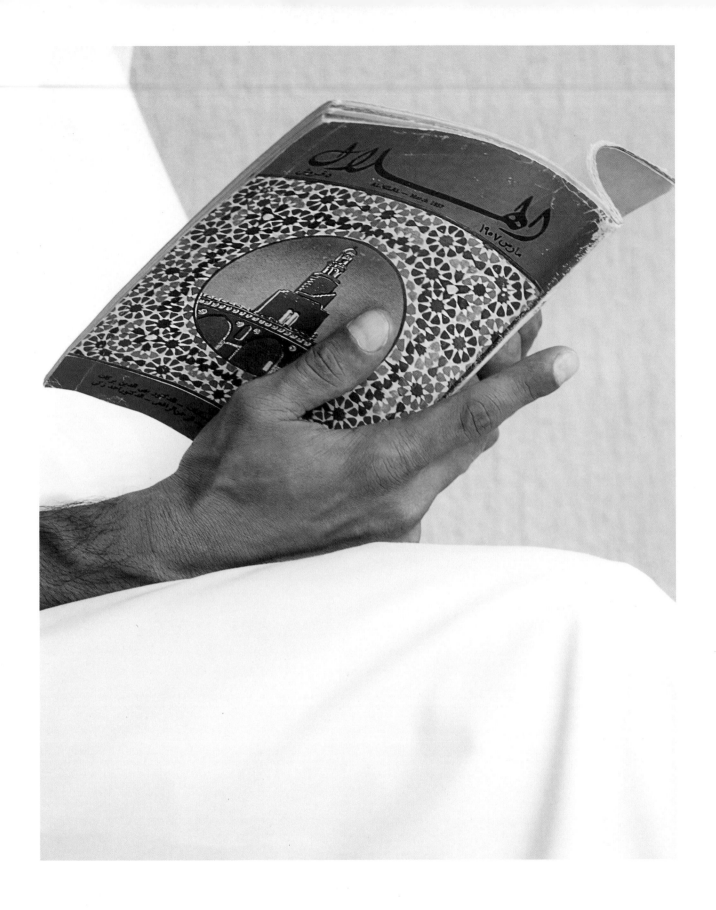

Brownbook magazine has been published for
over a decade. Its Dubai offices and satellite
projects feature custom-made furniture by
Case Design, a Mumbai-based architecture
and design firm.

Yves & Victor Gastou

"An entrepreneur is the offshoot of an adventurer," says Victor Gastou (opposite, right), who, along with his father, Yves, runs a chic Parisian gallery of decorative arts and design. "It's creative in the sense of having the ability to create—not necessarily originality." This drive, per Victor, necessitates both passion and a kind of willful madness: "a certain insouciance," as he puts it. "I've always admired entrepreneurs capable of amassing a fortune, falling into ruin, and making a fortune all over again," he marvels, citing Bernard Tapie, a French businessman who specialized in recovering bankrupted companies, as an example.

Victor initially studied economics and international affairs, only to circle back to the family business, where he's been working for nearly a decade. "Working with family surpasses normal familial relations," Victor says. "We're associates, friends, confidants—it's extremely enriching. There are no secrets." Moreover, father and son complement each other in key ways, deploying their personalities and tastes for their respective client rosters. The generational divide is an asset here: Yves' traditional view on the business balances Victor's contemporary take. "When my father needs to find a piece, he picks up his telephone. I pull out my computer," Victor explains.

Yves' early interest in art nouveau and art deco expanded after a whirlwind tour of Italy, during which he discovered designers such as Gio Ponti, Carlo Mollino and Carlo Scarpa. After years of selling design objects at a Parisian flea market, Yves landed his dream gallery space at 12 Rue Bonaparte, next to the eminent École Nationale Supérieure des Beaux-Arts.

The Saint-Germain-des-Prés neighborhood is known internationally for its art sellers and avid collectors. Yves commissioned Ettore Sottsass—celebrated for his vivid palette and elevation of inexpensive materials—to design his namesake gallery, which was the designer's first architectural project in France (and one of his first globally). The gallery has since featured modern icons such as Philippe Starck, Ron Arad, Tom Dixon and Shiro Kuramata, in addition to younger upstarts.

Habits have changed over the past years for sellers and collectors alike. As clients have left France, the Gastous have increased the number of international fairs they participate in to stay current and maintain regular client contact. Nonetheless, Victor says: "What one finds in Paris, one can't find anywhere else. It still holds a powerful place in the art world."

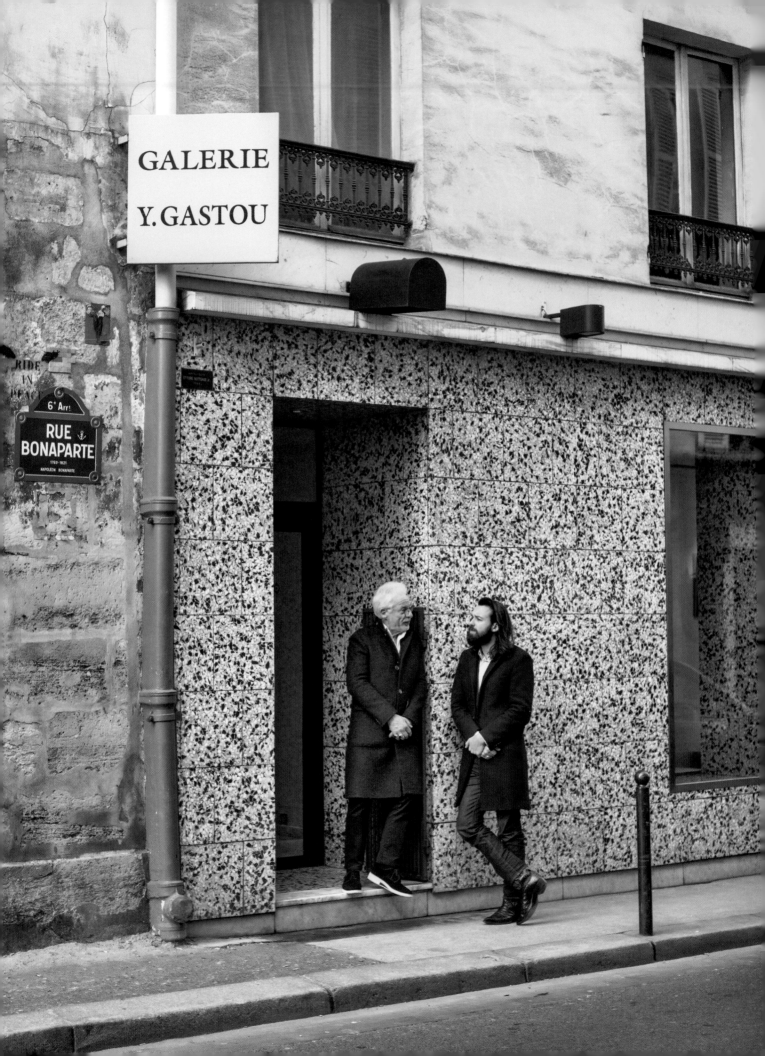

Above, left: In 2011, author Delphine Antoine
published *Yves Gastou Antiquaire du Futur* —
an illustrated monograph covering Yves' life
and what she termed his "radical career and
idiosyncratic taste."

PROFESSION:
RETAILERS

BUSINESS NAME:
KOLLEKTED BY

LOCATION:
OSLO, NORWAY

ESTABLISHED:
2013

Alessandro D'Orazio & Jannicke Kråkvik

Alessandro D'Orazio and Jannicke Kråkvik fell in love, moved in together and started their Oslo creative studio, Kråkvik&D'Orazio, within one week of meeting at a party in 2004. "We've been together almost 24 hours a day ever since," they say with a laugh.

Both Alessandro and Jannicke began their respective careers as interior stylists. When they met, they thought it would be better to join forces. Today, they continue to take on interior design and styling projects but focus much of their efforts on their retail venture. Their store, Kollekted By, opened in 2013 and offers the couple's favorite home accessories and furniture, including the duo's own collaboration with Danish design house Frama.

Though the business operates in a highly saturated market—Scandinavian interiors—Jannicke waves off any fear of competition. "We try not to look at what others do too much," she says. "Thanks to the internet and social media, we all get so entranced by other people. It's important to shut down and stop looking at everyone else. When you do that, you can think for yourself and have more fun."

When working on a big project, Alessandro and Jannicke will often take a few days offline to research. ("We still have to check our emails," Jannicke admits with a sigh.) Instead of using Google, the couple travels, reads books and visits museums for inspiration. Rarely do Alessandro and Jannicke look to other interior projects for ideas, however.

Kråkvik&D'Orazio is known for its playful use of color—a signature that differentiates them from the Scandinavian competition. Alessandro believes that his Italian heritage also helps sets them apart from what he calls "a typical Scandinavian style."

Living together allows Alessandro and Jannicke to be constantly on the job. They both emphasize the importance of restricting financial and administrative tasks to the office but otherwise seem to enjoy round-the-clock work.

"Our work is our life," Jannicke says. "It doesn't feel like work for us, though. We talk about it before we fall asleep, and it's the first thing we do in the morning. There's not much of a line between our private and professional lives. Sometimes that can be negative, but we're so happy and lucky to be able to do what we do."

"Don't be afraid to talk about work 24/7," Alessandro advises. "It means that you've found your passion."

"We collect all types of books—art, history, design, music—and always search for the best bookshops when out traveling," says Jannicke of the studio's robust library.

tricot
COMME des GARÇONS*

Above: A Comme des Garçons catalog
from 1984 offers a source of inspiration
for the duo. "We find beauty and inspiration
in the strangest things," says Jannicke.

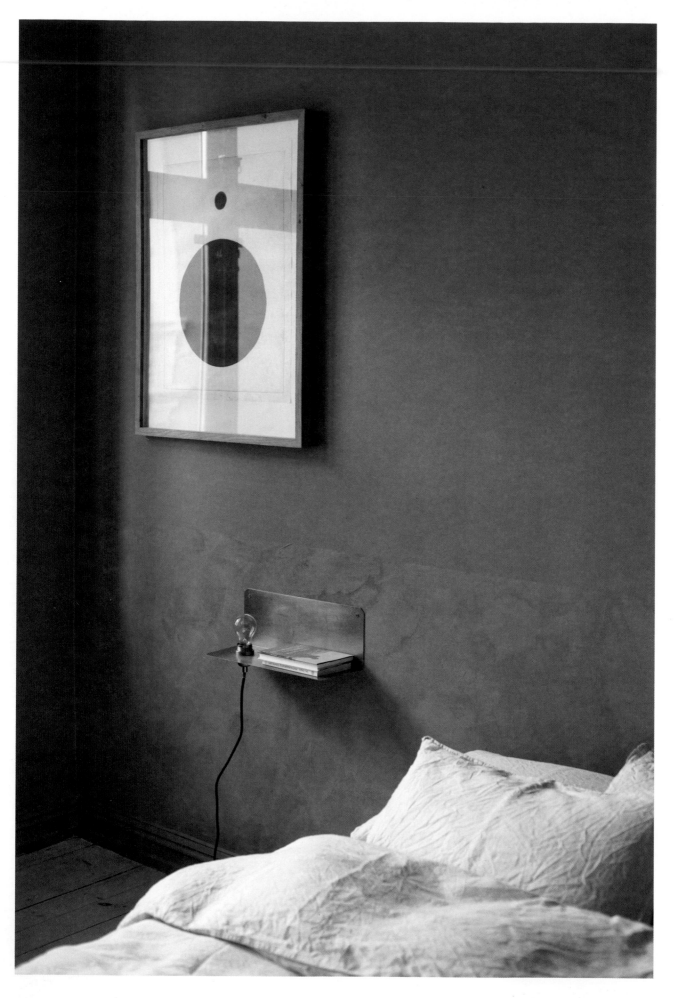

Jeremy Anderson & Gabriel Hendifar

When Gabriel Hendifar (opposite, left) and Jeremy Anderson began to experiment with lighting design, it was because they couldn't find anything suitable for their new home. The couple—self-confessed tinkerers—already spent their weekends perusing flea markets and decided to apply their DIY hankerings to a shared project. "He's an idea person and I like to make things, so he suggested that we start making some lamps," says Jeremy.

The duo is hazy on exactly when the art project morphed into Apparatus—their acclaimed design studio—but both agree that it was entirely unexpected. In 2011, a gallery-owner friend showed some of their designs on consignment. A blog picked them up, and by the time a restaurant group in Shanghai contacted them with an order, Apparatus had been born. By 2012, the brand had launched at contemporary furniture fair ICFF and the couple had moved from Los Angeles to New York, quitting their day jobs to focus full-time on the business. "We're definitely running on adrenaline," says Gabriel.

Take one look at Apparatus' sculptural lighting and it's easy to see how the brand attracted the attention of the interior design community with such speed. Gleaming brass shades, heavy porcelain chains and matte python-skin detailing lend the fixtures an appealing fluidity. While the collection boasts a few showstopping pieces, most are purposefully made to contribute less flourish. "They straddle a line between making you think a little bit and not demanding too much attention," says Gabriel. "We see what we do as just one ingredient for other designers to use when envisioning a space."

Now that they're presiding over a team of 40, the pair's respective backgrounds have proved pivotal to Apparatus' skyward growth. While Jeremy prefers solo, hands-on projects (in the early days, he crafted all of the fixtures), his background in PR lent him an invaluable knowledge of corporate infrastructure. Gabriel credits his experience working for womenswear designers JMary and Raquel Allegra as giving him a backstage pass to the creative cycle that takes an idea from abstract vision to successful commercial venture.

"One of the most important things that I think we do well, and this sounds so unglamorous, is knowing how to price a product," Gabriel

notes. "Ultimately, a lot of the things that we count as successful, that feel like they have a little bit of magic dust on them—like the fact we can offer a full suite of benefits to our employees, or that the business is profitable, and we don't have any debt—come down to making the right calculation about what something costs and how to bring it to the market."

"You've got to fight for the things that you believe in and make the things that you want to see," he adds. "The flip side is that you have to be serious about whether or not the world wants what you're making."

As business booms, the couple has learned to navigate the intense intertwining of their romantic and professional relationships. Work is never left at the office—particularly since Gabriel's most creative periods tend to happen late at night after Jeremy has gone to bed. "I'm barely rubbing my eyes and waking up in the morning when he'll be showing me all these things he's already drawn," says Jeremy.

"Now I know how to read the signs—whether or not he's interested in having that conversation at that time. The fights we get into aren't about differences in ideas as to how we should do things. They're about silly little behavioral patterns," says Gabriel. "They're couple fights!" adds Jeremy. "Yeah, we fight about stupid stuff," Gabriel agrees.

Occasional squabble aside, the duo's design perspective continues to forge a formidable presence in creative circles. They have rounded out the brand's offerings to include furniture and accessories—an Italian marble coffee table, triangular bookends and a porcelain incense burner. In 2016, they opened a spectacular studio in Chelsea to showcase Apparatus products against a coolly restrained, '70s-inspired backdrop that Gabriel describes as their "Yves Saint Laurent-Halston fantasy." The new showroom is exactly how the duo intends their designs to be viewed: not within a vacuum, but as one component of a stylish space.

Last spring, Gabriel and Jeremy decided to throw a party to celebrate their new studio; 800 people showed up to dance the night away. If Apparatus still needed proof of its success, it was right there. "That was the moment that I felt like, 'Okay, we just did it,'" remembers Gabriel. Or, as Jeremy puts it, "We arrived."

Apparatus' headquarters, a 10,000-square-foot floor-through on West 30th Street in New York City, comprises a workshop, showroom and offices.

Gabriel and Jeremy like to use materials
that evoke the glamour of the late '70s
and early '80s, such as aged or blackened
brass, tarnished silver and matte black
python skin. All leather used at the studio
is apparel-grade calfskin.

Apparatus' studio and showroom is also home
to the brand's assembly workshop and finishing
atelier. Everything is done under one roof.

Throughout the studio are contemporary art pieces, from wall sculptures by Robert Moreland to paintings by Mattea Perrotta. Gabriel and Jeremy's private office is shown at left.

Gabriel and Jeremy's designs
have been included in New York's Marlton
and Ludlow hotels and the Annabelle
Selldorf—designed Marta restaurant.

"You have to be serious about whether or not the world wants what you're making."

Tomas Backman,
Mattias Kardell
& Sven Wallén

"People feel better in places where they can be inspired, and where there's a purpose to everything surrounding them," says Tomas Backman (opposite, right), explaining the guiding philosophy behind Swedish real estate agency Fantastic Frank. Tomas—along with Stockholm natives Mattias Kardell (opposite, center) and Sven Wallén—founded Fantastic Frank in 2010. The partners' goal was to fill a gap in Stockholm's property market—one that called for a genuine interest in design and aesthetics.

"Early on, we were called 'the future of real estate.' Now, in developed markets such as Stockholm, the competition is copying us. It's great; competition is good," Tomas says. "Our idea was unique to the industry, and together we had interesting skills to offer," Sven adds. Despite different backgrounds and professional experiences, the three had always shared a passion for architecture, interiors and beautiful design.

Instead of renovating properties to a standard that would appeal to mainstream or mass markets, the Fantastic Frank team believes in creating something that perhaps only one person will ever truly love. It may seem like a gamble, but the model has set Fantastic Frank apart from its competition and allowed the company to double its office space in Stockholm, open an office in Berlin and make plans for a fourth elsewhere in Europe.

In a design-focused culture, the partners felt it only natural to create a brokerage agency that matched prospective owners with the perfect home. "A good match most often comes down to numbers, price and square meters. Those matches are usually fine, but we wanted to make it more soulful," Tomas says. "It disrupts the ordinary decision-making process behind buying property. Once you feel something for a space, you're more likely to open your wallet."

The company ethos took root in the home life of the three founders, where character seems to be the most coveted spec. "I love tables that bear marks from kids banging forks on them," says Tomas. "If you can see traces of life, then it's easier to live your own life in that space." The three fully believe that a home is more than just the sum of its rooms. Mattias says, "My home expresses who I am."

Since Fantastic Frank was founded, the team has collaborated with a roster of talented photographers, designers and stylists from the realms of fashion, interiors and architecture. They work together to showcase the properties as unique and enticing—just as they would appear in glossy magazines. The founders insist, however, that the company's mission remains authentic: It's about creating something from the heart. "Perfection makes us yawn," says Tomas.

"The normal rules of marketing a property
are the same as 30 years ago," says Tomas.
"Fantastic Frank has been a disruptive force.
So much so that even our competition has made
long trips to visit us."

"The competition is copying us. It's great; competition is good."

PROFESSION:
DESIGNERS

BUSINESS NAME:
RONAN & ERWAN
BOUROULLEC DESIGN

LOCATION:
PARIS, FRANCE

ESTABLISHED:
1997

Ronan & Erwan Bouroullec

If you ask Ronan Bouroullec (opposite, right), control is a quintessential part of being an entrepreneur. "I've never worked for anybody," the designer divulges. Complete independence, discounting his younger brother Erwan, of course, has allowed him to moderate the rhythm and quality of production at their studio. "There isn't a screw or cable that hasn't been designed by us," he says of their workspace. "We're behind each detail. We want to direct everything."

Ronan and Erwan grew up in the French countryside. Despite their parents' complete disinterest in design, Ronan muses that the brothers' business acumen, at least, is inherited. "In a certain way, I feel linked to my grandfather and the generations before him. They had a farm and did their own thing, selling potatoes and leeks," he says.

Commissioned right out of the gate by Italian firm Cappellini in 1997, their work was soon included in a group exhibition at the Centre Pompidou in Paris. Issey Miyake hired them to design a boutique; Vitra for a new office system. Last year, the Bouroullecs' latest projects were showcased across four tandem exhibitions in Rennes, the capital of their native Brittany.

The brothers' output ranges from product design to jewelry to interiors to urban planning. After two decades in business, the multiplicity of projects has not sparked a desire to scale up. "The goal is not to grow," Ronan affirms. "I'm not interested in having an assistant to think for me. I don't like meetings. I don't like to travel much. . . . The projects are small. You can't have too many—you have to make specific choices."

He continues: "What I don't like about the term *entrepreneur* is its financial connotations. I need money to do what I want, to be free, but that has never been the starting point for one of our projects. I need to be interested in the subject, and to work with people that are passionate too." Ronan describes their approach as akin to that of an auteur: "It has the same *écriture*, the same spirit, every time. Jasper Morrison, Konstantin Grcic—interesting designers always work in the same way. They are behind each millimeter of each project."

Working as a sibling duo alleviates the ups and downs. "We share thoughts about everything," Ronan remarks of working with Erwan. "The creative discipline is a mix of frustration and euphoria. You may feel you've got an extremely good idea, but after a few hours it's not so genius," he jokes. "You can feel depressed. But when you can share that, then it can help you restart. We're extremely lucky. You each give, and it grows from there. When something leaves the studio, it has to be considered good by both of us."

The studio, housed in a former factory in Paris' Belleville neighborhood, has "dust and mock-ups everywhere." "We would like to be more organized, but we aren't," Ronan admits. Recalling a recent visit from some rather corporate clients, he says, "If people want to work with us, then it means they must accept our process. We are digitally advanced, but we mix it with a knowledge of plaster, cardboard and Scotch tape."

Previous pages, left: At the Bouroullecs' studio, a graphic poster pays homage to Rennes, the capital of the French region of Brittany, where the brothers grew up.

PROFESSION:
ACCESSORIES DESIGNERS

BUSINESS NAME:
WANT LES ESSENTIELS

LOCATION:
MONTREAL, CANADA

ESTABLISHED:
2006

Byron & Dexter Peart

"This has been like therapy," jokes Dexter Peart (opposite, left). In the past hour, he and his twin brother, Byron, the urbane Canadian co-founders behind luxe accessories label WANT Les Essentiels, have covered the inherent power in being a twin, dreams of early retirement and adopting an attitude of fearlessness in the face of political and social change. The fast-talking duo is used to fitting a lot in: Over the course of the last decade, they have cultivated their fashion label into a sought-after brand that has grown to include a womenswear line, a men's shoe collection and a boutique in a brownstone in New York City's Greenwich Village.

Considering that WANT Les Essentiels was created with today's intensely mobile creative class in mind, it seems only fitting that one brother is in Montreal while the other has just landed in New York. "We've been traveling back and forth between New York and Montreal for the better part of 17 years for business," Dexter says, referring to their previous retail venture, WANT Agency, founded in 2000 to introduce Scandinavian fashion brands to North America.

It was with that international lifestyle in mind that they launched WANT Les Essentiels in 2006, seeking to capture a burgeoning corner of the luxury market with their range of sleekly designed, functionally minded products. The big fashion houses produced accessory lines already, but the brothers had spotted their niche: a brand that created timeless travel pieces specifically catered toward people on the go. "Most entrepreneurs are curious people who have noticed a void or opportunity in the market and have decided to go out and fill it in their own way," notes Byron. "It's a lot easier to have confidence when it's the two of us," Dexter adds. "It helps us pass through fear and anxiety to try something that's meaningful and exciting and relevant."

They view their range of elegant totes, holdalls and backpacks, as well as leather passport cases and toiletry bags, as practical tools to support the lives of their jet-set clientele. "I'd like to think that our customer is very discerning," says Byron. "They expect and anticipate having very well-considered things around them because their life is already frenetic and they want it to have a little more order to it." When Maria Sharapova posted a series of photographs to her Instagram account, black WANT Les Essentiels backpack in hand as she raced from airport to sporting event to hotel room, the duo was delighted. "She's using it in her everyday and that was

Previous pages, left: Twin brothers Byron and
Dexter stand in front of WANT Les Essentiels'
West Village boutique in New York City.
Left and opposite: The brand's various products.

really important to us," observes Dexter, who says they have never gifted
her with any products. He sees these moments as proof that their target
demographic—successful, design-oriented and always on the move—has
naturally adopted WANT's accessories as a companion in their lives.

Byron and Dexter—whom their elder brother wryly refers to as the
"mutual congratulation society"—are buoyant conversationalists, their
words tumbling together as they discuss their unusual dynamic as business
partners and twins. "We feel kind of guilty," Byron says with a chuckle of
the envy that their closeness can inspire in others. Dexter adds, "There's a
really awesome competitive spirit between us, but we're on the same team."
Naturally collaborative, they have always shared the spotlight, bounced
ideas off one another and employed a healthy serving of sarcasm. "I think
we have a mutual denigration society too—we bring each other down as
much as we lift each other up," says Byron. His twin explains, "It's very
much a relationship—one side business partnership, one side brothers,
one side married couple."

In their partnership, Dexter assumes the role of the realist, his cool-
headed pragmatism balancing out Byron's wilder idealism. Their visions
for the path ahead often diverge, but there is a profound comfort in knowing that regardless of how they get there, differing ideas are underwritten
by the same set of values. "It's a little bit like using Waze," says Dexter,
referring to the community-sourced traffic navigation app. "Sometimes
we're going on the route that Byron suggested, other times we're going on
the one that I suggested, and occasionally we compromise and combine
our two different routes into one."

Even as their stock rises, the Pearts are loath to slow down. When their
flagship store launched in New York, it symbolized the fruition of decades
of dreaming. But it was back to business as usual the following day. "I remember being in a hotel that night and thinking, 'We just did what we've
been dreaming of doing for all these years, and we didn't even celebrate or
enjoy it,'" recalls Byron incredulously. "I'd love to enjoy the moments more."

Opposite: The twins pride themselves on the
homey feeling of their boutique in New York
City; patrons are invited to relax into a pair
of 1965 Dezza chairs by Gio Ponti.

Mette & Rolf Hay

For Rolf and Mette Hay, who run contemporary Danish furniture and accessories company HAY, work does not stop at 6 o'clock every evening. For this husband-and-wife team, their business is their hobby and creating high-quality design at affordable prices is what drives them.

Their designs lie at the intersection of architecture, art and fashion. Where Rolf focuses his boundless energy on the slow burn of furniture design and production, Mette brings life and motion into the accessories lines. Mette sees opportunities for design everywhere—from toothbrushes to matchboxes. Meanwhile, Rolf turns introspective for days, emerging with a brilliant idea for a chair that can take the next three years to turn into a beautifully crafted reality. They each respect what the other brings to the company; they are the answer to each other's questions.

Mette and Rolf grew up not far from one another in Jutland. Mette knew from a young age that she wanted to get into design—her parents' furniture store was a second home to her. For Rolf, it was when he moved to Germany in his early 20s and just happened to land a job in a furniture shop that he was introduced to the likes of Charles and Ray Eames and Arne Jacobsen. He would spend weeks reading about design, often driving five hours to the Vitra Design Museum on weekends.

They met while working for Danish design house Gubi and, along with their business partner, Troels Holch Povlsen, soon pooled their talents to create HAY. When they were first starting out, Rolf would set his alarm for 4 a.m. and be at the factory by 7: Meeting the day head-on is something he still holds dear. They opened their first shop in the heart of Copenhagen; while other furniture companies based themselves outside the city, they opted for a smaller space, finding the constant dialogue with their customers to be invaluable.

The Hays create democratic design in the spirit of Bauhaus, making furniture that customers will still want to live with—and which hasn't fallen apart—years later. They also believe that sustainability is essential for the future of the furniture industry as a whole.

They now have over 20 shops around the world but will not open stores just to grow the brand. It needs to be done in the right way, in the right space and, most importantly, with the right people. Entrepreneurship has never been about money for the Hays. It's about passion. "When I think of an entrepreneur, I think of passion and energy—someone who's eager to achieve something. And perhaps it also helps to be a little bit stupid and naive. You can think of the best idea in the world, and then you can think of 10 reasons not to do it," says Rolf.

Above: Mette and Rolf examine some of
HAY's pieces at the brand's product
development studio in Copenhagen.

"It helps to be a little bit stupid and naive. You can think of the best idea in the world, and then you can think of 10 reasons not to do it."

HAY's flagship store is in central Copenhagen, but the brand is expanding with a series of HAY Mini Markets (bazaar-like stores selling a tightly edited curation of everyday objects) from New York to Shanghai.

3:

Creating a Community

To foster, serve and strengthen: a company is like any community.

PROFESSION:
ARCHITECT

BUSINESS NAME:
JOSEPH DIRAND
ARCHITECTURE

LOCATION:
PARIS, FRANCE

ESTABLISHED:
1999

Joseph Dirand

Joseph Dirand's stark design articulates sumptuous essentials. Slender and garrulous, the Parisian-born-and-raised architect delivers French opulence with great restraint, accentuating both the past and the ultramodern for projects in France (the Rosenblum Collection in Paris, the Villa Pierquin in Saint-Girons) and abroad (a Saifi penthouse in Beirut, the Distrito Capital hotel in Mexico City).

For nearly two decades, Joseph's studio has been highly sought-after for creating spectacular settings for luxury labels. He feels that this success is a result of prizing quality over uniformity. He explains, "We're living at a time when risk is something people don't like—they only copy what's been done before. Developers will spend on what they know will sell. It's a visionary who says: 'Yeah, but maybe there are people who will be happy to pay more to have something much better.'"

Joseph's professional headquarters is a luminous sixth-floor perch on Paris' Right Bank with an unobstructed view over the city's rooftops. The open-plan workspace for his staff of 25 is trimmed with neatly arranged groupings of every kind of material sample, and his personal office is equipped with a full library of art and architecture books and his favorite Jeanneret chair.

Joseph readily discusses his architectural icons, including Carlo Scarpa and Ludwig Mies van der Rohe. He runs his fingers through his salt-and-pepper hair often and briskly strokes at his stubble—the only twitches in his otherwise polished command of who he is and what he does with his striking visual vocabulary.

All of Joseph's designs start with references from movie scenes, books and other iconic designers. When he launches a project, he begins by revisiting his own bookshelf. For a new building in LA, he consulted photographs by Ed Ruscha to get a time-specific vision of modernism. For a project in the Bahamas, he drew inspiration from traditional Japanese dwellings, which were adapted into colonial-style bungalows.

To remain devoted to these projects that can often take many years to realize, he says he has to want to invest his whole life into the process. "The rhythm is very extreme," he notes of the commitment to his business, the travel and the ceaseless finessing. Moreover, he says, "I need people who challenge me—I like it when my clients are difficult with me, exigent, so if I sometimes feel a little lazy, they will reawaken me." (*continued*)

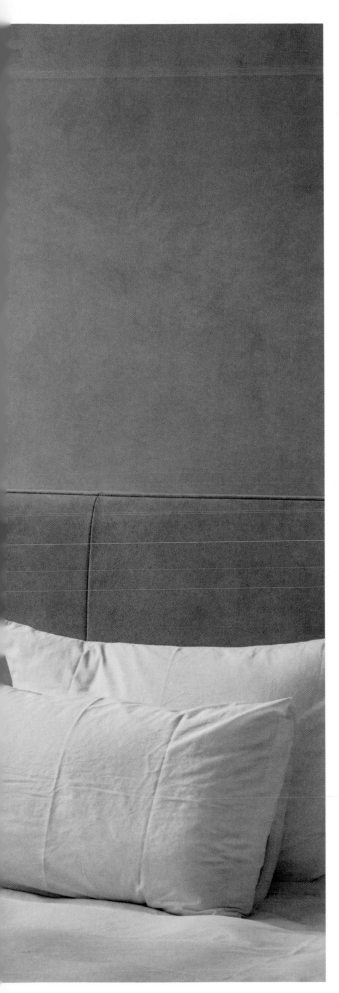

He continues, "It's important to collaborate with people who drive the project in the same way as you. Little by little, you find those people and work with them again. And then you almost don't need any other clients."

Such great partnerships are knitted together through a mutually liberal and trusting spirit. "I need to love my client, and for them to love me as well," Joseph says. "Selectivity means you work with people who give you more freedom, who give you the opportunity to develop extraordinary things."

Joseph's thoroughly experiential approach to his field and his business means he's involved in aspects well beyond the scope of the mise-en-scène of a room: He reviews the logo, the website and the playlist corresponding to the spaces he works on. He tastes the food with the chef at the restaurant, he does complete mock-ups of suites and tests the bed for hotels.

He equates his exacting approach to meeting his client's needs with a dandy's sense of meticulousness. A dandy, he remarks, "has style, but he has his own style, and he pays attention to every single detail, aesthetically, to create a beautiful life. He cares about everything." To maintain such an integral vision, "we work with visionary people," Joseph says. His rigor about quality informs the clientele he attracts: "I prefer to know that my clients—my community—will be sensitive to where they're going to live. That's what I care about."

Joseph's passion for perfectionism is obvious: "We love when it's difficult. We love to prototype—we want to design everything: the handle of the door, the taps; we are even thinking of working with brands to customize fridges. You need to find challenges that force you to go further and further, and explore and be amazed by the result. We do it until we get every proportion right, every color."

"My design is not only about a certain look. It is about life. People will sit next to each other, work at the table, have sex; it will be amazing. All of this is important," Joseph says of his work.

Above: Marble frequently factors into Joseph's design process. Shifting his attention to large-scale public projects has allowed him to extend the reach of his vision into larger communities.

43
Volume Manor, 1965/2003
Gelatin silver print

44
Linton Terrace, 1965/2003
Gelatin silver print

Above: Joseph sits in Loulou, a restaurant he
designed for Paris' Musée des Arts Décoratifs.

"I need people who challenge me—I like it when my clients are difficult."

PROFESSION:
HOTELIER

BUSINESS NAME:
COQUI COQUI

LOCATION:
YUCATÁN PENINSULA,
MEXICO

ESTABLISHED:
2003

Francesca Bonato

"My mother says that when I was young, my backpack was always ready to go," says Francesca Bonato. "I've always wanted to see how other people live, to find out what other places are like. I just have an inexplicable urge to go everywhere."

Francesca's desire to travel first took her on a solo adventure from her native Italy to Mexico to explore the nation's landscapes. While there, she met her husband, Nicolas Malleville (he served her coffee on one of Tulum's white sandy beaches). The two quickly fell in love, married and started to work toward a shared dream: founding Coqui Coqui—a mini hotel empire on the Yucatán Peninsula.

Francesca recalls, "Our friends and family all started coming to stay. We decided to build a guest room, and then another one. We kept adding more, and our home started to become a hotel." But she points out that Coqui Coqui grew from humble beginnings: "Nicolas and I didn't have money when we started, so I would cut papayas for everyone's breakfast while he was out cleaning the beach." She continues, "We dreamed it all up and built it together from nothing."

Today, Coqui Coqui's boutique hotels are bohemian hideaways that can be found in Valladolid, Coba and Mérida. Francesca and Nicolas work hard to ensure that each hotel reflects the culture and customs of its locale. "When we move into a new city, we work with its community. We invest in its people and learn any traditions. It's not just opening a hotel—we work to earn the trust of local residents, and are able to infuse each hotel with elements of its surrounding culture and history as a result," Francesca says.

One aspect of the Yucatán Peninsula that the duo particularly welcomes is the region's natural tropical scents. So much so that each Coqui Coqui hotel has a personalized fragrance thanks to the couple's perfumery. There's dewy coconut inspired by Tulum's beaches, lime and mint to reflect Coba's lush gardens, and a strong scent of dried roses to reflect the town of Valladolid. The perfumery is what Francesca refers to as the soul of the business. "It's the true essence of the hotel," she says. "Nicolas loves perfumes, and goes out in the jungle, exploring the flora everywhere we go." The scents are meant to be transporting, urging the wearer to escape to a more relaxed and simpler way of life while at the hotels. "Our clients can feel everything that we put into our hotel and perfumery. They can sense that it's all made with passion," says Francesca. "We set out with love as a driving force, and we've learned that people understand it."

Above: Francesca mixes local herbs,
flowers and woods for the perfumery's
Sabores collection. Opposite: The Spa at
La Perfumeria in Valladolid.

Francesca and Nicolas create a new fragrance
for each hotel they open, inspired by the
local environment, culture and vegetation.
The motivation is to allow guests to connect
with nature and local communities.

PROFESSION:
FASHION DESIGNER

BUSINESS NAME:
MINÄ PERHONEN

LOCATION:
TOKYO, JAPAN

ESTABLISHED:
1995

Akira Minagawa

Akira Minagawa may have named his fashion and textile label Minä Perhonen after the Finnish for "the wings of a butterfly," but his business ethic remains grounded in a far less ethereal belief in good old-fashioned hard work. "Don't be lazy, don't give up, and treat customers and business associates well," he says, recalling advice he absorbed from his grandparents, who ran a business importing European furniture to Japan. They are lessons that have stood Akira in good stead: Since the designer launched his brand in 1995, his fashion, fabrics and homeware business has grown to include 11 shops across Japan and stockists around the world.

His slow and steady approach to craftsmanship mirrors the unwavering pursuit of his ambitions. "I don't just have a single goal. They are dotted like a starry sky, so I spend my time looking up at each star and making an effort to get closer and closer each day," he says. At 19, Akira visited Scandinavia for the first time and was entranced by the region's pragmatic lifestyle and understated approach to style. A newfound aesthetic appreciation was infused with his own design ideals—a winsome composite that can be seen in the playful patterns, jaunty neckerchiefs and outsize bowler hats in the uniforms Akira designed for the staff at the Tokyo Skytree building. "We hope that people who wear our clothes simply feel happier," he once noted. More recent leaps toward the stars include a new one-stop shop in Tokyo's Spiral building and a collaboration with Finnish furniture company Artek at Helsinki Design Week in 2016.

Now the boss of over 100 employees, Akira shrugs off his own accomplishments. But he admits that it does feel meaningful to spot signs that his business is having a lasting impact. "You can feel the work gradually penetrate into society," he explains, pointing to a pattern he designed 17 years ago that is not only still used by his own business today, but is also used by a Danish textile company and a Japanese furniture company. "We feel that our most important contribution to making things is shown clearly when a design has a long life," he adds.

When difficulties crop up, Akira's implicit trust in the future gives him a sense of perspective. "Things don't always go smoothly—they go at an irregular speed—but they will surely reach a landing point someday," he says. "So even when you feel that things have stagnated, don't panic. Confront what you have to face."

Whether he's finding business solutions or designing a new pattern, Akira gets most of his ideas when he's drawing.

Akira cuts into a swath of fabric embroidered with what he refers to as his "tambourine" pattern. The textile was first released in 2000 and has stayed in production for 17 years.

243

"When you feel that things have stagnated, don't panic. Confront what you have to face."

Angela Oguntala

Angela Oguntala helps companies to prepare for an eternal unknown: the future. Through what she describes as a blend of strategic foresight and design, she helps businesses to not only forecast potential challenges and opportunities but also to create and manage change—to choose the futures they want to work toward.

Her approach is based on the principle that in the same way our visions of the future inspire us, they can also start to limit us. A company's scope of possibility, she says, can narrow when the company is fixated on a specific goal. One must, she advises, "define a vision for where you want to go and be acutely aware of how quickly your plan can fall apart."

When studying Angela's CV, one cannot help but notice that her advice to others—to imagine alternate realities—is reflected in the unpredictability of her own practice: Her meetings are scattered across the globe, and her schedule is punctuated with trips to Los Angeles, Atlanta, and London, where her office is located. The clients she consults for include urban planners, health-care companies and film producers. She once lived in Iran, and cites Caribbean science fiction as an inspiration.

Such an unfettered disposition is what led Angela to future studies in the first place. "Someone once called me a futurist at a conference, and I looked around trying to figure out whom they were talking about before realizing it was me," she says. What might have been a throwaway comment became the beginning of a newly reimagined course for Angela, who had, up until that point, worked in business strategy. Based on her own beginnings, Angela suggests budding entrepreneurs "ask questions that aren't being asked and go from there."

The need to think ahead is what invigorates Angela's ambition. Holding the belief that one should prepare for alternate futures rather than succumb to daunting Orwellian notions of them, she advises anyone considering a change of direction to do the following: "Write a letter to the future you. Use it as a moment to reflect on what you've done for yourself. We never take the time to validate our actions. It's a powerful experience."

When in Copenhagen, Angela prefers to work at cafés in the neighborhoods of Islands Brygge and Christianshavn. "I like being by the water," she says.

In 2014, Angela was named a "Future Innovator" by the Austrian cultural, educational and scientific institute Ars Electronica.

Efe Cakarel

It was in a beautiful café in Tokyo's Roppongi Hills in 2007 that Efe Cakarel first had the idea for MUBI, his curated online cinema platform that allows people in over 200 countries to watch extraordinary movies. He was in the nation with the world's fastest broadband and what was then the world's third biggest film market. And yet he couldn't watch a film online.

Entrepreneurship is in Efe's DNA: his first job as a tea-boy in his father's company meant that he was already overhearing conversations about business strategy as a 10-year-old. So, not one to sit and wait for a gap in the market to be filled, he started writing a business plan on the flight back to San Francisco from Tokyo. "Nothing happens unless you focus all your energy on it," he says, "unless you jump with your entire body."

While he acted on his idea relatively quickly, the journey to that point has deeper roots. Efe remembers his childhood in the coastal Turkish city of Izmir, visiting the art-house theater with his mother on Saturday afternoons. If he closes his eyes, he can still picture it. It was there that his love of cinema began, where *Cinema Paradiso* first moved him, where his Fellini obsession blossomed.

But film wasn't his only passion, and it was his head for numbers—he was on the Turkish national mathematics team—that led to a scholarship at MIT. In 1994, while studying there, Efe first experienced the brilliance of directors like Wong Kar-wai instead of just the big names whose films had made it to his corner of Turkey. By the time he finished college, he was so in love with cinema that he knew he had to somehow make it his life.

At first, he tried to make films—after a stint at Goldman Sachs, he spent time in Paris writing a script. But it was obvious to him that he wasn't going to be the best. And if he was going to make films, he wanted to be as good as the best. MUBI, he believes, can be the world's premier destination for cinema. Crucially, unlike Netflix, it hosts only the greatest films—a new

When MUBI almost went out of business, Efe sought advice from a board member. "He asked: 'Do you still have the energy? The number one rule of business is to stay in business. Do whatever you have to do.'"

one every day, each available for 30 days. So it provides a constantly rotating library of remarkable works from the likes of Xavier Dolan, Andrea Arnold and Ann Hui.

Efe has chosen 20 tastemakers from around the world to select the roster. He thinks of them as curators—just like the person who created the Rauschenberg exhibit at the Tate Modern, he explains. MUBI is growing fast, and expecting a million plus subscribers in a couple of years. And MUBI is beginning to acquire films straight from festivals. Efe is confident that within the next 10 years, if you want the latest release from the Coen Brothers or the newest movie from Almodóvar, you'll find it on MUBI.

MUBI operates from an 18th-century town house in London's Soho neighborhood, with beautiful wooden floors and big central tables. While Efe expects hard work from his colleagues (if people start leaving before 8 p.m., he can start to feel like he's hired too many people, he says), it's an approach based on love, not fear.

But for all Efe's innovation, one thing has remained the same since his childhood in Turkey: his breakfast—a soft-boiled egg, tomatoes with olive oil, and bread with butter and jam. It's the little things that matter, even for big thinkers like Efe.

PROFESSION:
ARCHITECT

BUSINESS NAME:
FRIDA ESCOBEDO

LOCATION:
MEXICO CITY, MEXICO

ESTABLISHED:
2006

Frida Escobedo

Mexican architect Frida Escobedo co-founded her first studio, Perro Rojo, at the tender age of 24. Upon going solo in 2006, she quickly began stacking up awards and recognition for her work, and it wasn't long before she found herself flying back and forth and designing in both the United States and Mexico.

Over a decade later, Frida is becoming weary of having to deal with the "practical" side of architecture: the budgets, the deadlines—all of which she considers too cold and calculated. Still, whether it's a hotel, a gallery or a public space, her work continues to convey energy—a bold blend of modernism and Mexican tradition.

"Architecture isn't an easy discipline," Frida says. "It takes a lot from you, and it's not the most lucrative career. It's challenging to try to keep a practice with projects you believe in that also covers the payroll every month."

Her office is on a quiet street in the Anzures neighborhood of Mexico City, just a few blocks away from her home. "I'm lucky enough to walk to work," she says. "My partner's office is also halfway between the house and my studio, so we often have lunch together, but if we don't, I usually eat with the guys from the office. It's a small team, so I feel like they're part of my family."

The creative process that Frida enjoys with her co-workers makes juggling the logistics of running a business worth the effort. "There's a period when you get a 'Eureka!' moment that's filled with adrenaline, then you start doubting if it's really a good idea at all," she says. "There are definitely moments when I don't think before I jump. I don't think it's adrenaline as much as it's passion. I associate adrenaline with risk or competition, whereas passion is about endurance and resilience."

Running her own business affords Frida a certain level of spontaneity. "I guess that's one of the reasons I chose to have an independent practice," she says. "It's hard to keep reasonably healthy finances, and there's a lot of stress to deal with, but it allows me to create my own path. I also think that in order to remain spontaneous, you have to stay curious and not get too comfortable. [Belgian architect] Kersten Geers once told me you need to 'stay slippery,' otherwise you stop learning and growing."

When things don't go well at work, it's Frida's role to keep spirits high and maintain a positive energy at the studio; there's no room for self-indulgence or complaining. "You need to move on and make room for something else," she says. "But there are so many highlights. You learn to be resilient, to enjoy things as they come and to stay flexible and open. If you enjoy the things you do, you stop seeing it as work and start seeing it as a way of life."

Frida opts for superfine MUJI and Pentel
Sign pens while sketching out new ideas
for projects and proposals.

Following pages: Frida won a competition in 2010 to turn the former home and studio of muralist David Alfaro Siqueiros in Cuernavacai into a cultural hub for the local community.

"I associate adrenaline with risk, whereas passion is about endurance and resilience."

PLAZA

FRIDA ESCOBEDO

Above: The bookshelves in Frida's office are designed by Derek Dellekamp. Some of her favorite books include *The Production of Space* by Henri Lefebvre and *The Human Condition* by Hannah Arendt. The frame on the second shelf features her favorite photo of her mother.

Apollonia Poilâne

"Entrepreneurship bears a lot of resemblance to baking bread," says Apollonia Poilâne. As chief executive of Poilâne—a bread empire with an international network of retailers and six shops in Paris, London and Antwerp—she ought to know.

"Entrepreneurs take simple ingredients like the water, flour, salt and yeast—or, in our case, sourdough—that we use for baking and, with their know-how and a team, turn them into something bigger than the sum of the individual parts or people," she explains.

When Apollonia's parents died in a helicopter accident in 2002, the then-18-year-old was left in charge of the family business that her grand-father had founded in 1932. "I had two options," she recalls. "I could hire someone to take on the management of the company. Or I could run the business I had grown up with—that I knew inside and out."

She chose the latter, and operated Poilâne from her Harvard dorm room for four years before she moved back to Paris. Now she lives just down the street from the bakery's original location on Rue du Cherche-Midi and manages the operations side of Poilâne. But she also works regularly in the bakery. She emphasizes how important it is for the business that she stay connected to its craft—making bread.

"When I first started, my business card read 'CEO.' Still, many people were convinced that my role was merely social," Apollonia remembers. "That made me so mad. I decided to add the word *baker*, and now I'm tempted to take away the 'CEO' title altogether."

When asked what advice she would give to young business owners, Apollonia stresses the importance of carving out personal time. "Honestly, I haven't done that enough," she admits. "I've been extremely fortunate, in that I was able to go to university and study economics. I'm also lucky to have such great friends, but all of this—losing my parents and taking over the company—did take a toll on my youth."

Apollonia doesn't lament her lack of free time for long. Sitting in her office, surrounded by paintings of Poilâne's famed miche loaf, it is evident that she deeply loves what she does. "You have to have an appetite for your business," Apollonia asserts. "That hunger is so important. It helps you to overcome all of the little things that try to get in your way."

Giving Paris its daily bread is a family endeavor. Apollonia's uncle, Max Poilâne, runs three of his own bakery locations in the French capital.

PROFESSION:
MANUFACTURER

BUSINESS NAME:
SEVEN UNIFORM

LOCATION:
TOKYO, JAPAN

ESTABLISHED:
1952

Tokuji Motojima

Have you ever slipped into your work clothes and immediately felt better equipped for the day ahead? According to Tokuji Motojima, the CEO of Seven Uniform, that's no coincidence. The psychological impact of this transformation is what he's built his global business around.

"Workwear should act as an on-off power switch," he says. "For example, a cast member at Disneyland once told me that even when she woke up with a severe hangover, she changed when she put on her uniform—just like someone had flicked her switch into work mode."

Tokuji's company, which was founded in 1952 by his father-in-law, has tapped into this behavioral insight to create work apparel that places employees' identities at the heart of their designs. Its premium line of uniforms, HAKUÏ, was launched by Tokuji in the 1990s to address the shifting needs of businesses, which had started to recognize that confident employees lead to better customer service. Tokuji—whose own uniform is the suit he puts on every morning—is an earnest advocate for the morale-boosting qualities of well-considered workwear. The trick, he believes, is placing the employees' comfort first.

"Most employees complain about conventional work clothes or brand-name work clothes provided by their employer, and that's probably because they were designed without thinking carefully about workers," he says. "Therefore, we now have to think about the worker's identity—not the company's."

Tracing the history of the work uniform in Japan, Tokuji identifies three key phases that have led to the current trend in high-quality, design-led staff uniforms. First, there were the purely functional smocks and coveralls that defined Japan's spectacular postwar economic boom. That period of practicality was followed by a flashier phase of big-name fashion designers who added their logo to brands, but with little thought to the needs of those who wore the clothes each day. The final stage—which laid the groundwork for Tokuji to launch HAKUÏ—is known as *hataraki-gi*, which loosely translates to "clothes that make your neighbors feel happy and relaxed." (*continued*)

HAKUÏ workwear has been designed exclusively by Akira Onozuka since 1992. Every year, 20 new designs are developed; after 25 years, 500 designs have been created so far.

"They are special compared to other uniforms. They are made with craftsmanship and give workers a professional appearance," says Tokuji. Current HAKUÏ offerings include a black overall dress, a double-breasted coat with cheekily striped cuffs and an oversize knee-length top with a belted waist. Tokuji and his creative collaborator, Akira Onozuka, are careful to approach workwear designs with the same care as they would for ordinary clothing—both, they believe, should focus on first-rate materials and comfortable cuts. "The basics of workwear are very much the same as the basics of clothing itself," Tokuji adds.

Throughout the business's expansion, he has followed the mantra of his late father-in-law. "Do not imitate others. Be yourself," he says, pointing to the newly developed "C-train" fabric, made from recycled winter coats, as proof of HAKUÏ's freewheeling identity. Adaptability is essential, as is the humility to recognize when change is needed. "In the case of economic crisis, it's necessary to check if the business method is good or not," he says. "The business's methods become obsolete over time, so I have to renew them periodically."

A considered and thoughtful man, Tokuji feels that his business is inextricably linked with both his own spiritual practices and his country's precise cultural codes. His latest goal of raising the basic salary of his manufacturers bucks Japan's existing wage hierarchy. Here he's applying the traditional principle of *sanpō yoshi*: a win-win philosophy that—much like the company's workwear uniforms—emphasizes the importance of the employees' satisfaction for business success.

"I'm always telling my employees to work joyfully, visit customers often and retain their trust, impress them with our work, and create ties with them," he explains of the incentivizing effects of such an ambition on his staff. "This way, I believe that everything will be good in the end—the company, the customer and the world."

Robert Klanten

"I've always been at the top of the food chain," says Robert Klanten, founder and CEO of Die Gestalten Verlag—the German publishing powerhouse that has churned out 500-odd books since 1997. From titles on typography, logos and branding to coffee-table tomes on visual culture with mass appeal—anything from tattoos to travel—Klanten and his team produce 40 new publications annually, to a tune of 10 million euros each year.

The company's Berlin headquarters are sleek and seem to hum like a well-oiled machine. In a small meeting room, Klanten recounts how he built the business from the ground up. Once a humble graphic designer, he took pains—and three years—to acquaint himself with specific areas of the business (sales, distribution, accounting), building each department himself before leaving someone more qualified in his wake.

"I've never had a boss in my life," he says, more apology than brag. "Everything I've done has been based on whatever I thought could be done, should be done, or else what I would be interested in." And this mind-set translates to his definition of entrepreneurship: "It's very much about being empowered to follow your own ideas and building a business around them."

In 2016, a Gestalten retail expansion stalled and failed to secure a line of credit. Klanten was looking at what he described at the time as "a large hole in his pocket" and a personal liability that could have put him in jail. The company voluntarily filed for insolvency—a shrewd move that sidestepped its creditors.

Following a restructuring, Klanten has refocused Gestalten's efforts on publishing. Today, its books continue to be sold for around 40 euros a pop in 100 different countries, and the company maintains offices in London, New York and Tokyo. After two decades in the business, Klanten still rolls up his sleeves and works hard. He leads by example, in a style he describes as demanding: "I need to be. That's the only way to keep things going," he says.

As a colleague, however, Klanten prides himself on being approachable and is humble about his responsibility in the company: "I always try to improve how I'm doing, how I could be more concise and how I can be more of an inspiration for everybody else so that they respect me."

Despite the company's peaks and more recent troughs, Klanten views his enterprise as "a long-distance run without a finish line." That may sound like a slog—Sisyphus eternally rolling a boulder up a hill—but Klanten's motivation is unerring. "Success, I feel, is to be able to live a decent life, have fun and take pride in what you do." It has, he says, never really been about money: "Here, success means creating value—whatever that may be—for like-minded people. That's very satisfying indeed."

Since 2003, the publishing house has also run
its own foundry, Gestalten Fonts, and offered a
selection of over 150 typefaces, display fonts and
experimental fonts created by and for designers.

PROFESSION:
RESTAURATEUR

BUSINESS NAME:
LIFE

LOCATION:
TOKYO, JAPAN

ESTABLISHED:
2003

Shoichiro Aiba

As the son of deli owners, Shoichiro Aiba has always known that good food has the power to bring people together. In Tokyo, his Italian restaurant, LIFE, has nurtured a sense of community amid the city's 13 million inhabitants since it was founded in 2003.

Shoichiro opened his restaurant in Yoyogi-Hachiman—a quiet residential district near his home. At the time, the area lacked the hustle and bustle of neighborhoods like Harajuku, but Shoichiro had a hunch that its proximity to one of Tokyo's largest parks might attract diners. "When I visited Italy, I preferred to drop into cafés near a park or a market—they were always filled with customers," Shoichiro explains of his inspiration. "I think those attractions are what draw people, rather than the restaurant itself."

He started publishing a free magazine and produced a handmade map of the local area. LIFE's location and menu were included, as were those of the neighborhood's other restaurants—a simple but savvy piece of marketing that underpinned Shoichiro's vision of a united, growing community.

As LIFE flourished, so too did other local businesses, until the area began to draw curious visitors from other prefectures. The once low-key neighborhood has transformed into a fashionable enclave for artists and third-wave coffee shops, in large part due to Shoichiro's foresight. "The area has a new trendy name—Oku-Shibuya—and is becoming an attractive place for people to hang out. We talk about ourselves and get to know each other," he says of the sense of camaraderie found at his restaurant—which now boasts a self-published cookbook, not to mention four offshoot restaurants (LIFE Son, LIFE Niigata, LIFE Sea and LIFE Daily Meals).

While Japan has had an obsession with Italian cuisine for decades, it has been slow to appreciate another aspect of Italian life—a fondness for the sweet pleasures of self-indulgence. Quite the opposite, in fact: Japan's unforgiving work culture has gained such traction that the term *karoshi* entered the national lexicon in the 1980s to describe sudden death from overwork. Shoichiro, who headed to Italy after high school to hone his sauce-making and pasta-rolling skills, however, actively seeks to integrate Italians' appreciation for family and free time into his business model.

"Give priority to your family, and leave work on the back burner," he once noted in an interview when recalling the lessons he learned during his time in Italy. "That way of thinking had a profound effect on me." In practical terms, this translates to Shoichiro encouraging his staff to take time off for family commitments, while he treasures the simple routines of daily life with his own wife and their two children.

LIFE enjoys citywide popularity, but Shoichiro is especially pleased to welcome a crowd of mostly local customers who return again and again: "Regular customers are our backbone," he says. Their loyalty is rewarded through the occasional free glass of wine or complimentary dish in a system that Shoichiro leaves entirely to his staff's discretion. "'The more you come, the more you get,' is our service policy because we'd like to increase our fan base and regular customers," he says. LIFE also hosts larger community-based activities, like the summer festival Mochi-tsuki, during which sweet boiled rice is pounded into a Japanese treat called mochi. "I'm so happy that people are pleased with these events," he adds. "LIFE itself is my contribution to the community."

In the vastness of Tokyo, Shoichiro has carved out the intimacy of a small town. Daily Japanese specialties from his father's delicatessen are served alongside Italian dishes; the sweet radishes and seaweed are an accommodation to the more traditional tastes of older patrons. Despite LIFE's international cuisine, Shoichiro hopes he's created the easy atmosphere of a neighborhood cafeteria. "When I was a little boy, local people recognized me as the son at my father's delicatessen," he says. "I think my son is seen by my customers in the same way. I'll be glad if I could continue to be regarded as 'Shoichiro from LIFE.'"

In 2016, Shoichiro joined forces with Need
Supply Co. to open LIFE Daily Meals inside
the fashion brand's Kumamoto store. Even as
his empire expands, he still makes time to get
involved in the kitchen.

Shoichiro regularly organizes live music
events for the local community. The flyer
pictured above is for a solo musician
who performed at LIFE Son.

"Give priority to your family, and leave work on the back burner."

Juan Maiz Casas & Marie von Haniel

Entrepreneurial endeavors can be difficult to pull off in remote locations. In Tasmania, however, isolation only serves as a boon for Marie von Haniel and Juan Maiz Casas—the couple behind Piermont Retreat.

Operating Piermont undoubtedly comes with its challenges; the nearest town on either side is 40 minutes away. But Juan and Marie believe that the demands of owning a business in rural Tasmania are less an impediment than an opportunity to flex some entrepreneurial muscle.

They see running Piermont as a chance to build on the vision of Marie's father, who founded the company, and say that entrepreneurship is in their blood. "It would be pretty much impossible for me to go and work for someone else's company. I can't stop thinking about what's next," Juan explains. "It's a 24/7 exercise. It's quite exhausting, actually."

The couple has created a resort that meets their exacting standards in sustainable design. As Marie says, "We see ourselves as part of the environment and believe we have a right to be there. In the long term, our impact isn't huge because we're building something that doesn't need replacing for another 200 years. That was my father's philosophy too."

Sustainability extends beyond architecture for this entrepreneurial couple. Juan and Marie's three children are already thinking about whether they might like to stay in the family business. "It's not our dream that one of the kids will take over," Juan explains. "If it happens, great. But right now, we're getting the business up to a size where it can run well without us having to be so hands-on. As the kids get older and need more experiences than Swansea can offer, we'll need to be a bit more mobile."

Conscious of their own needs as much as of their children's, Juan and Marie know that operating a hotel may not work for them forever: "There's a burnout period in hospitality. There are only so many years you can face guests. It's not as hard as, say, [running] a dairy farm, but we're tied to this place."

Marie's advice to those just beginning an entrepreneurial journey is simple: "Look after your employees and do your homework," she says. Juan says firmly, "You have to do it yourself because no one will do it for you. When you really want something, no one else will go the miles on your behalf. You're the only person who can get you there."

Opposite: The hotel overlooks Tasmania's
Great Oyster Bay. Piermont was envisioned
by Marie's father as a small community of
sustainably built lodgings that would
coexist with its natural surroundings.

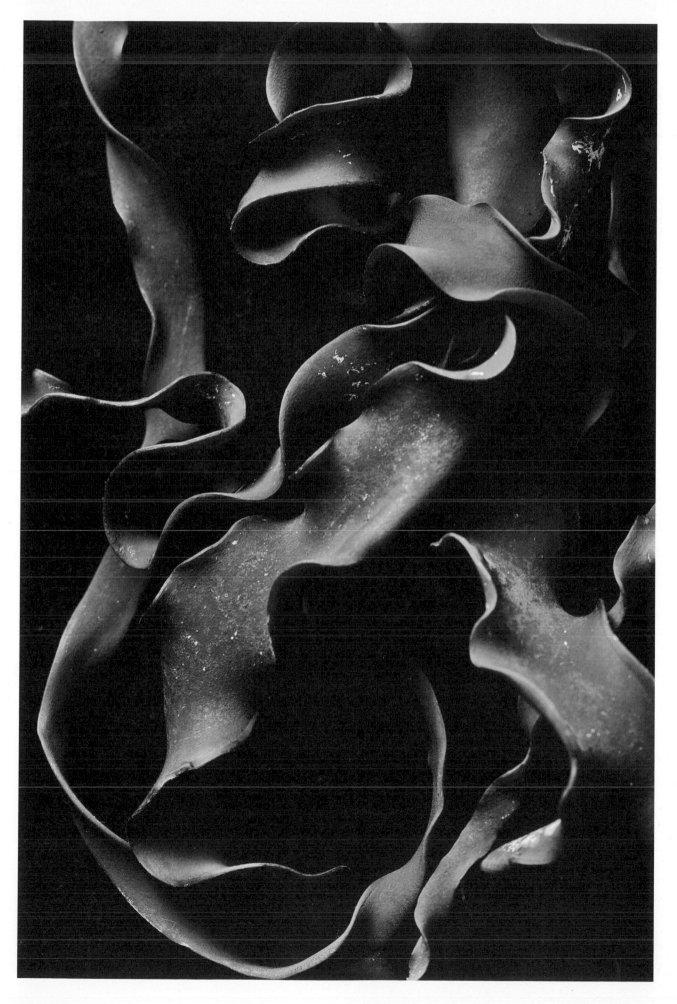

4:

Tips

Expert advice and wise words from more entrepreneurs.

How To: Hire Properly

Hiring has become less about skill than about likeability and "cultural fit." Yscaira Jimenez founded LaborX to help fix hiring blind spots, and the platform has been critical for the job searches of nontraditional applicants. From job descriptions to interview questions, she says, the entire hiring process should be broken down and reconceived in ways that accurately predict performance and promote diversity, both for the company and on a grander scale. Passionate about changing society through changing employment opportunities, Yscaira talked to Charles Shafaieh about the problems experienced by companies due to a homogeneous staff, the importance of merit-based hiring and how ensuring the diversity of your company can never begin too soon.

CHARLES SHAFAIEH: *What do you see as the biggest problems with hiring practices today?*

YSCAIRA JIMENEZ: Using practices—such as referrals and looking at college degrees—that are not necessarily predictive of whether someone is going to be successful or not. When you rely on those metrics, you miss out on a lot of great potential talent that might be just as good or a better fit. It also leads to homogeneous workforces, products and companies. McKinsey put out a report saying that there's a business case for being more inclusive and that more diverse teams outperform teams that are more similar.

CHARLES: *"Good fit" has a shifting definition. In America, it seems that managers are hiring based not on an individual's ability but on the degree to which he or she satisfies an idea of "cultural fit." Many people ask themselves questions such as, "Would I want to be stuck in an airport with this person?" I assume you're against this way of thinking?*

YSCAIRA: I am a fierce opponent of it and have built a company that provides an alternative.

CHARLES: *Which is a move toward meritocratic-based hiring.*

YSCAIRA: Correct.

CHARLES: *What other platforms or resources should entrepreneurs be looking at when they are going about the hiring process?*

YSCAIRA: The traditional tools have some value, but they are also restrictive. For example, LinkedIn is skewed toward the professional class, primarily with college degrees, but

WORDS:
CHARLES SHAFAIEH

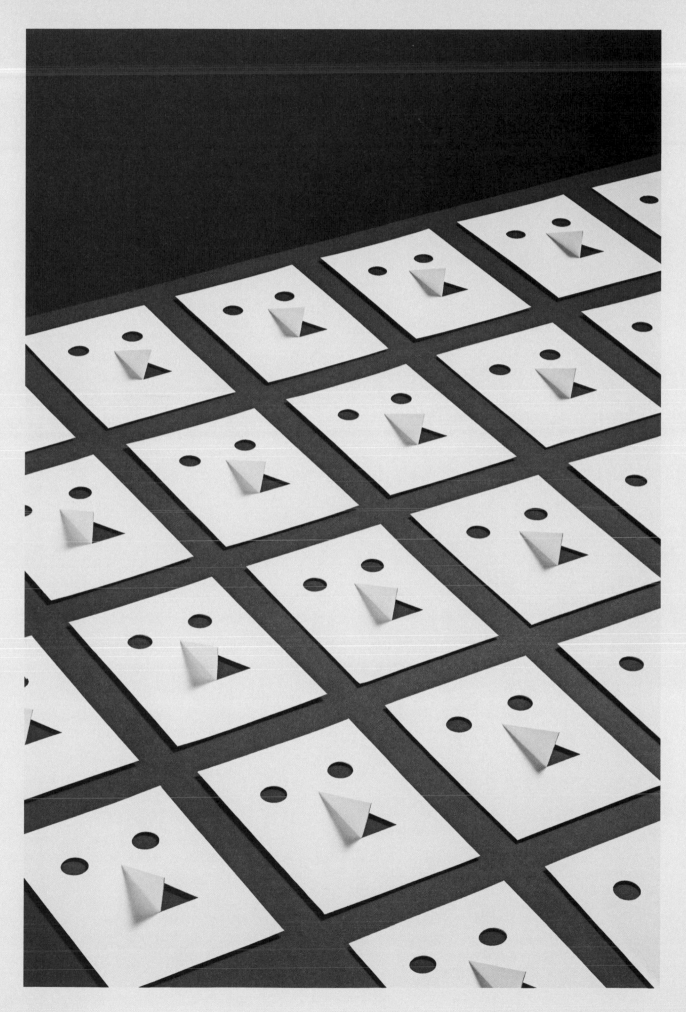

two-thirds of our workforce does not have a college degree. Focus on the way you hire, such as your interview questions and process. Google used to have people solve brainteasers but dropped it because there is no correlation between knowing how many marbles there are in a jar and whether you are going to be good for a role.

With traditional candidates who are recent graduates, you'd ask questions like, "What clubs were you a part of?" "How many leadership positions did you hold?" What you are looking for is initiative, interest and passion, and there are other ways to ask those questions. Someone who hasn't gone to school could be volunteering at their local church, they could work at a nonprofit, or they might be the go-to person in their neighborhood. You can ask questions in a different way to recognize leadership, initiative and these other criteria.

For example, if a candidate is coming out of a boot camp or a training program, talk about what they've learned in those three months or six months or a year. Or dig a little deeper to learn about on-the-job experience: A customer service representative didn't really think she had work samples, but her customers had reviewed her on Yelp. I think this is very important information for a hiring manager—more important than things you put on your résumé.

CHARLES: *It's a way of rethinking the notion of what makes someone qualified, for employees and employers.*

YSCAIRA: Do you really need a four-year degree to do sales, IT or software development? You don't! You can learn these skills in many other ways. Rewriting job descriptions to make them as open as possible, redefining hiring processes and taking a hard look at the "culture fit" issue are important.

Ultimately, I need to know if this person could ask me for help or if I could ask this person for help if I need it—things that are relevant to the work and that will make this person successful in the organization. Think about whether a person

brings a perspective you don't have that can give your product a wider reach or tap into a new marketplace.

CHARLES: *Rethinking hiring in this way changes how people self-select when considering the jobs to which they might apply.*

YSCAIRA: Exactly. You may want to consider putting your interview questions on your company's website. Some people come in a lot more prepared for interviews, but that may be an issue of social gap, not an issue of ability or fit for that role.

CHARLES: *On the subject of interviews, what are your thoughts on blind hiring practices, like symphony orchestras have used for a long time? Some people advocate for anonymity.*

YSCAIRA: Ultimately that candidate is going to have to show their face and present their voice. But it might help them to get further along in the process.

I am actually a proponent for being really intentional about being more diverse and inclusive. Instead of anonymizing everything, you should look at the product, your customer base, your demographics and the culture in which you want to be building your company.

I think that the real business implications are that homogeneous companies are probably not building the best, most profitable products. Over a billion people are on Facebook, but maybe if things started a little bit differently, there might be 3 or 4 billion. At Apple, an all-male engineering team built the health app, and they aren't building for health issues that affect half of the world's population. That's a big missed opportunity.

You should have a team that represents your customer base. And if the customer base is really diverse, like America, then you should be building very diverse products.

CHARLES: *Should entrepreneurs with very small companies go about this process in a different way than a huge company like Google or Apple?*

YSCAIRA: The earlier you do it, the bigger the opportunity you have. When I think of companies like Google, they are

"Google used to have people solve brainteasers but dropped it because there is no correlation between knowing how many marbles there are in a jar and whether you are going to be good for a role."

such a massive organization, but they haven't been able to move those numbers in a significant way. It is still 1 percent black and 3 percent Latino.

I don't think you should do anything differently when you are a start-up. Sometimes we need to pull in friends and people with whom we have worked, so our networks are limited or homogeneous. It just means we have to work a little harder. I can rely on my network, but if I am a white male, then I should realize that it is imperative that I reach beyond my network for support or for people who can bring bigger pipelines. If you're looking for an engineer or a software developer, look at organizations like Women Who Code. Say you are looking for a diverse team, then you encourage everyone to apply—but especially women, people with disabilities, and black, Latino, and other underrepresented folks.

CHARLES: *This is a broader call for people, whether they are starting a company or not, to expand their social circles. If they find themselves in a hiring position later, they have already become part of a diverse community rather than just small, monocultural circles.*

YSCAIRA: The stat I've heard that floored me is that the average white male has worked with 1 percent black co-workers. There are many static issues that drive this, but there are things that we can do to step out of our bubbles.

When people think about where they should move or where they should go to school, there are not many out there who really value having diversity as one of the criteria for the search.

So when I think about the schools to which I want to send my unborn children or the type of neighborhood to which I want to move, sure, there is convenience and what I can afford. Beyond that, though, is seeing whether it is a diverse community. Something more personal that we can all do is take responsibility for where we choose to live, to work, to go to

school, and to think about how integrated the community is. When you are in a position in a company in which you have to do team-building activities, think outside the box of what you would normally do and find other ideas. I might like the outdoors and hiking, but maybe other people prefer barbecues or just playing a game.

There are a lot of things you can do and think about that would create ways for you to interact with other people.

CHARLES: *Deutsche Bank claims that an algorithm, when used in searches through potential-candidate pools, will help fix their diversity issues. Can this be part of the solution too?*

YSCAIRA: I heard a quote once that resonated with me: How can you trust the people that created the problem to create the solution? I'm a big believer that this problem is going to be solved in part by technology and algorithms, but I think these algorithms should be built by a more diverse group of people so that they are not perpetuating the bias already out there. I think we are all trying to crack this problem. We might all be doing something very similar, or we might be doing something very different. Companies sort of protect their algorithms with their lives, so it is hard to tell if it's really different or not at this point.

Whoever has better resources has a higher probability of succeeding, so that's another issue that gets into bias. We need to change how funding is allocated so we have more diverse entrepreneurs building the solutions.

CHARLES: *The larger argument you're making is that when we start changing the way we live in our communities, the companies we create and the products we make—and therefore our customers—will start to benefit from these experiences.*

YSCAIRA: Relying on the government to do what's right and what makes sense can take generations. But you create opportunity when you hire, and that accelerates this inclusion that I am talking about.

How To:
Lead People

The opposite of leadership isn't anarchy, it's plain old management. That's what Bob Chapman says he realized when he took over his family's failing bottle washing business in 1975.

Chapman, who is now one of America's most sought-after leadership consultants, paints a bleak picture of what the workweek looked like at Barry-Wehmiller when he became CEO: Employees at the St. Louis plant started work when a bell rang, took breaks when they were told to and were assigned to the same task every day. He and the other bosses sat in their offices and barked orders.

"I thought my job was to manage people—that we were smarter and brighter, and that people would come to us and we'd tell them what to do," recalls Chapman, who is now in his seventies.

The story of what happened next has become legendary—a case study touted by motivational speakers and pored over by business students around the world. Chapman started letting employees choose when to take their breaks, and unlocked the equipment stores that had previously been kept guarded. He encouraged everyone to express themselves honestly to their superiors, and adjusted the new policies accordingly when they did so. Profits skyrocketed: Barry-Wehmiller grew into a conglomerate of 80 companies and counting, worth over $2 billion in 2017.

"We always knew good leaders knew how to talk, but we've discovered that the greatest attribute of leaders is the ability to listen," Chapman says when asked about the turnaround. "Leadership means making sure that you are being a good steward of the lives entrusted to you and treating those people as somebody's precious child."

Today, this hardly seems like a radical intervention. Chapman's definition of leadership as stewardship is just one of a dizzying number in circulation, and perhaps even a somewhat old-fashioned one: Comparing employees to children would raise eyebrows today. But the fact that his workplace policies were, not so long ago, considered a staggering break with business as usual is a reminder of just how recently the field of leadership studies has asserted itself. Chapman recalls his

WORDS:
HARRIET FITCH LITTLE

own 1960s education with contempt: "I took management classes, got a management degree and a job in management. I was never taught to care for anybody." Half a century on, leadership is lauded as the most important skill that entrepreneurs need to acquire. US companies alone spend over $14 billion annually on leadership development; colleges offer hundreds of courses on the topic; several publications put out hotly anticipated annual lists of companies ranked according to how well they equip employees to become future leaders.

What changed? It seems that for much of the 20th century, the way we thought about leadership fell outside the purview of teachable experience. Academics who were interested in the topic trained their energy on identifying the personality traits of successful leaders—Benjamin Franklin's collaborative nature; Thomas Edison's curiosity; Henry Ford's emotional intelligence. This was an application of the so-called Great Man Theory of history: the idea that some people have been endowed with particular qualities that allow them to amass a loyal following, and that the key to understanding their success lies in identifying what exactly those qualities are. While academics buried their heads in history books, managers—Chapman among them—were taught the simple, uninspiring skills of administration.

In the 1980s, it became increasingly clear that the Great Man Theory was getting researchers nowhere. The orthodoxy shifted: Leadership, it was now contended, could be learned. As Warren Bennis, a pioneer in the field, concluded grandly at the turn of the 20th century: "The most dangerous leadership myth is that leaders are born ... do not believe it. The truth is that the major capacities and competencies of leadership can be learned if the basic desire to learn them exists."

This approach has been in the ascendance ever since and with it, a pressing new concern: If leadership can be taught, what should we be teaching?

One of the most enduring ideas is the one that Chapman sensed instinctively in his bottle washing plant: Good leaders reap the benefits of ensuring that employees feel loved and trusted. Today, the greatest champion of this approach is Simon Sinek—the British-American author whose 2009 TED Talk, "How Great Leaders Inspire Action," is the third most viewed of all time.

According to Sinek, leaders who make people feel safe create an environment in which risks will be taken, concerns voiced and mistakes owned up to—all necessary attributes of a dynamic company. As he put it in one recent presentation, "When a leader makes the choice to put the safety and lives of the people inside the organization first ... so that the people remain and feel safe and feel like they belong, remarkable things happen."

Sinek leans heavily on evolutionary biology to make his case. He speaks about companies as "tribes" and explains that, like cavemen afraid of the saber-toothed tigers lurking in the darkness nearby, we instinctively value alphas who make it their priority to protect the pack. He also uses military analogies. Why is it, Sinek asks, that we laud the officers who sacrifice themselves for others on the battlefield but reward bosses who act selfishly in the boardroom?

Such allegories—and leadership gurus are particularly fond of them—should be approached with healthy skepticism. Companies aren't caves, and employees aren't soldiers. But the assertion that a feeling of safety can boost performance is easily verifiable.

Chapman's leadership of Barry-Wehmiller is a striking case in point. In 2008, when the recession hit and the company lost 30 percent of its orders overnight, he decided not to implement layoffs but created a furlough program instead. Every employee had to take a month of unpaid leave within the year, but they could choose how they broke up the time and trade it with others if possible.

According to Chapman, not only did the company come out of the recession ahead of competitors, but productivity and morale also saw a huge bounce. His conclusion: "Our decision to use furloughs to save jobs made our associates proud and profoundly touched by the realization that they worked for a company that truly cared about them."

Some leaders have taken this philosophy even further. In 2012, the e-commerce company Next Jump introduced a "no-fire" policy: Unless employees behave unethically, they can't be sacked. CEO Charlie Kim (who has also adopted the title "Chief Officer of Happiness") told journalists at the time that he was implementing the policy to foster a sense of long-termism within a fast-moving digital economy where employees often fretted over job security.

It worked. When the no-fire policy was introduced, the percentage of employees who said they loved their jobs jumped from 20 to 90 percent, and turnover shrank from 40 percent to almost zero.

Sinek, who uses Next Jump as a case study, draws the following conclusion in his book *Leaders Eat Last*: "People would rather feel safe among their colleagues, have the opportunity to grow and feel a part of something bigger than themselves than work in a place that simply makes them rich."

Sinek's hugely popular approach signals a sharp departure from the Great Man line of enquiry—policy, not personality, is what he thinks drives success.

But not everyone agrees with the idea that good bosses should promote a feeling of security.

Cy Wakeman, a Nebraska-based keynote speaker and best-selling author, most recently of *No Ego*, is a disruptive voice in this sphere.

"Entrepreneurs will go broke trying to buy happiness," she says dismissively when asked about Sinek's philosophy. "I was happy all day Saturday and I got nothing done. Happiness doesn't drive productivity."

Wakeman argues that while the safety-first approach may work on the factory floor, white-collar, digitally driven businesses require less coddling. "The world's really different today," she says. "People come with their own mind, their own computer, their own smoothie. It's not about what we give

them to buy their love—our job as a leader has grown into helping people evolve."

Wakeman, who calls her approach Reality-Based Leadership, believes that the way a leader can help employees evolve is by fostering extreme self-reliance. Rather than attempt to perfect the work environment, a good leader should teach how to rise above circumstances and succeed regardless.

She hit on this approach while working as a counselor, a sphere in which she says it was normal to encourage clients to find ways of dealing with the cards they had been dealt rather than dream of alternate realities. Why, she wondered, couldn't we apply the same tough love in the office?

Her advice to leaders is to ditch open-door policies and be quick to fire difficult employees. "Drama is emotional waste, and the job of a leader is to eliminate waste through good processes," she says. She thinks that it's a particularly important lesson for women to learn: "Women have been conditioned to think that we're responsible for other people's happiness ... but the best use of our time is to implement our business plans and ideas and really wean people off relying on us."

Wakeman's approach is, by her own admission, "very contrary"—a direct provocation to current trends. And while she can readily cite examples of companies whose performance has improved under her tutelage, there are good reasons to question her assertion that people naturally thrive in environments of self-sufficiency. One US Gallup poll from 2013 found that 40 percent of people who are ignored by their boss will actively disengage from their work, while only 1 percent of those who are recognized for their strengths will do so.

Gia Ganesh, a member of the Forbes Coaches Council, has been weighing the options for several years now. She comes down against the idea that bosses should distance themselves

> "People come with their own mind, their own computer, their own smoothie. It's not about what we give them to buy their love—our job as a leader has grown into helping people evolve."

from their employees: "People leave bosses, not companies, and if people leave their bosses, it's because of a lack of engagement between the leader and employee," says Ganesh.

She argues that far from being old-fashioned and factory-focused, bosses who promote positive work environments are particularly important for fast-growing businesses, especially start-ups. "There's a big focus on innovation today, but you need to create an environment of trust where innovation can happen inherently," she says. "Trust comes from empowering people to do things while knowing that they're not going to be reprimanded for it."

Wakeman does, however, make an important argument about the importance of sincerity. A key problem that she identifies is that many organizations pay lip service to the idea of responsive leadership and open doors with no real substance. This, she argues, is far worse than doing nothing at all: "We tell [employers] that they should let people vent, but I actually found that that increases negativity ... engagement without accountability creates entitlement."

"Leadership," the American historian James MacGregor Burns wrote in 1978, "is one of the most observed and least understood phenomena on earth." The problem he was referring to was an intellectual one—his discipline's failure to make any real headway in its understanding of why certain figures had successfully inspired revolutions and led armies.

But recently, the same argument has been made again. Barbara Kellerman, the founding executive director of the Harvard Kennedy School's Center for Public Leadership, shocked colleagues in 2012 when she published *The End of Leadership*, a provocative book in which she argued that contemporary leadership teaching was contradictory and confusing and rarely delivered results.

"Leadership programs tend to proliferate without objective assessment; leadership as an area of intellectual inquiry remains thin; and little original thought has been given to what leader learning in the second decade of the 21st century should look like," she wrote. And then she went on to suggest that the useful field of enquiry would be the study of followers, as their experience was the more common one: "Thinking about leadership without thinking about followership is a fool's errand."

There is, of course, an irony to the way Kellerman moved so rapidly from dismissing the leadership industry as dead to suggesting a fix-all solution for its woes. But her observation that studies of leadership would do well to move toward followership has proved accurate.

Even the recent omnipresence of buzzwords like "company culture" is evidence that we now hold organizations up to far more democratic standards than was previously the case. Followers, not leaders; policies, not personalities: The entrepreneurs who crave industry recognition in coming years will have to prioritize others in order to get it.

In Ganesh's opinion, some people will always be better suited to being in charge, but for a company to flourish, it must give as much weight to the well-being of its employees as to that of its bosses. "That is the basic tenet of any human relationship—with your parents, your kids, your colleagues," she says.

Ganesh says that a line by civil rights activist and poet Maya Angelou has influenced her thinking on this: "People will forget what you said, people will forget what you did, but people will never forget how you made them feel." It is, perhaps even more importantly, a sentiment that holds true outside the nine to five.

How To:
Manage Mistakes

We all make a lot of mistakes. Some of them will matter in the long run, but most of them won't: Forgetting a meeting or realizing we've entrusted a project to the wrong person is the type of problem that will most likely resolve itself with time and a few carefully worded emails. So why can it still feel like the end of the world when we fail at something? Are there ways we can learn to handle our mistakes that don't involve anxiety, self-recrimination and wasted time? Alain de Botton, philosopher and founder of The School of Life, wants us to change the way we think about things going wrong. In conversation with Harriet Fitch Little, he advanced some unconventional solutions—including embracing self-pity and becoming imaginary friends with ourselves—and explained why our "faulty walnuts" (that's our brains) so often fail us when it comes to failure itself.

HARRIET FITCH LITTLE: *In your writings about love, you emphasize that romantic relationships are often imperfect—full of mistakes, revisions and times when we're really just muddling through. Is it the same with work?*

ALAIN DE BOTTON: If we were forced to describe a successful life, it might go something like this: We pick just the right area of work early on, swerve neatly into new fields at the ideal moment and get public recognition, money and honor for our efforts. To our surprise, despite our education and apparently realistic and practical natures, such scenarios occur about as often as winning the lottery. We don't grasp just how rare and strange 90 years on earth without major disasters in love and work might actually be. Our brains—the faulty walnuts through which we assess reality—have a habit of fatefully misunderstanding statistics. We imagine some things are much more common than they really are. We might suppose that half of new businesses are a great success. In fact, it is less than 2 percent.

HARRIET: *Is there a way to make our "faulty walnuts" better at accepting this reality?*

ALAIN: If we could really see what love and work were like for most other people, we'd be so much less sad about our own situation and attainments. If we could fly across the world and peer into everyone's lives and minds, we'd perceive how very frequent disappointment is, how much unfulfilled

WORDS:
HARRIET FITCH LITTLE

ambition is circulating, how much confusion and uncertainty is being played out in private and how many breakdowns and intemperate arguments unfold with each new day. And then we'd realize just how—statistically speaking—abnormal and therefore cruel the goals we have set ourselves really are.

HARRIET: *When we realize we've made a mistake, the first feedback we get is from the inner voices in our head. Generally, that feedback is negative. Why are we such hard taskmasters?*

ALAIN: We don't often think about it—and may never discuss it with others—but pretty much everyone has voices in their head. Not in any disturbing way: just the murmuring stream of thoughts that runs along inside our minds most of the time. Sometimes the voice is more explicit, encouraging you to run those final few yards to finish a race, for example. But sometimes the inner voice is simply not very nice. It's defeatist and punitive, panic-stricken and humiliating. It doesn't represent our best insights or most mature capacities. We've internalized the voice of a harassed or angry parent; the menacing threats of an elder sibling keen to put us down; the words of a schoolyard bully or a teacher who seemed impossible to please. We absorbed those unhelpful voices because at certain key moments in the past they sounded compelling. The authority figures repeated their messages over and over until they got lodged in our way of thinking.

HARRIET: *Can we coach these voices to be more helpful?*

ALAIN: To change our inner voices, we need to encounter an equally convincing and confident, but also helpful and constructive, variety of voices over long periods. We need to hear them often enough and around tricky issues so that they come to feel like normal and natural responses. Eventually, that will be how we talk to ourselves; those will become our thoughts.

HARRIET: *Is it ever okay just to wallow?*

ALAIN: Self-pity is regarded as a rather awful failing, and anyone caught up in it must be forcibly reminded how very lucky they are. How dare our children moan about having to do homework? Don't they realize there are other children with terrible diseases who'd love to be doing math homework? Haven't got a job you like? Stop moaning: Think of people working the Ndassima gold mine in the Central African Republic.

But to better deal with self-pity, whether in ourselves or others, we have to keep in mind something that this well-meaning—but sadly ineffective—strategy misses. It's that self-pity starts out as a very important achievement. Imagine what things would be like if we couldn't pity ourselves. If you think of a parent comforting a child, they are in effect teaching the child how to look after themselves. Gradually, we learn to internalize this parental attitude and come to be able to feel sorry for ourselves when no one else will. It's not necessarily entirely rational, but it's a coping mechanism—a first protective shell developed to manage some of the immense disappointments and frustrations that life throws at us. The defensive posture of self-pity isn't inherently contemptible. It's grounded in something rather touching and useful.

HARRIET: *A protective shell sounds like a good first step, but how can we move beyond self-pity?*

ALAIN: It's not in the least surprising that we try to keep very painful facts about our own inadequacy and failure at bay. The issue is how one might slowly evolve away from self-pity, and here the answer is that it's possible only in a supportive and gentle atmosphere. Very few of us improve our characters by being shouted at. Self-pity is wisely addressed not by condemnation but by the kind suggestion of better perspective and fair criticism: Perhaps one did do something a little wrong, perhaps this won't seem like such a problem tomorrow morning. If this can be taken on board, then the need to ward off failure or to avoid responsibility is lessened. Self-pity is no longer required. We learn through reassurance, not bracing reproof—however precise the condemnation may be.

HARRIET: *One of the hardest parts of making a mistake is when it impacts other people. How should we approach apologies?*

ALAIN: It's very important to be ready to say sorry—and to apologize with genuine contrition. Modern society often tells us that we should learn to feel good about ourselves. Enough of having to feel ashamed of who we are and what we do. But religions don't agree. All of them carve out moments in the calendar when they expect us to take stock of the bad stuff we've done, all the unthinking evil and carelessness we're responsible for—and then they ask us to say sorry. Religions accept that all of us are "bad." The question is whether we are

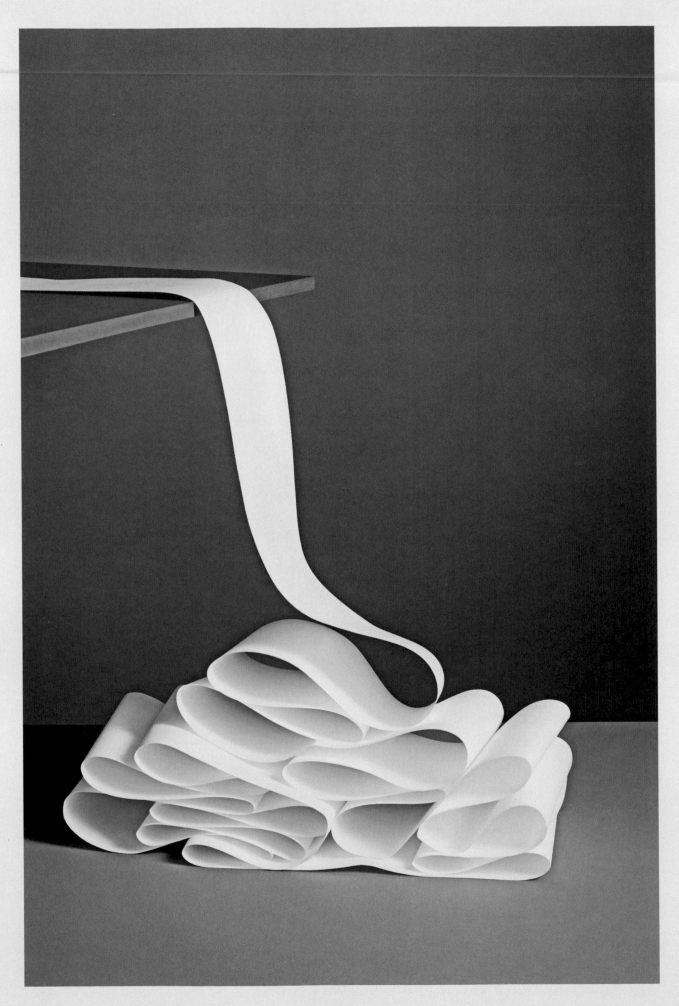

> "We need to make ourselves totally at home with failure, rather than attempt to evade it. Pessimism has a bad reputation, but it is one of the kindest and most generous of philosophies."

able to rise above our awful sides, acknowledge them and say sorry for them. We should look back over our behavior and do that most unfamiliar and pre-modern thing: atone. That is, we need to apologize for what an idiot and low-key monster we've been over the past few months. A public invitation to atone is meant to encourage us to inch toward moral improvement. Thinking one is great and kind all the time is simply not a good basis for actually being so. Whatever you think of religion, it understands this bit of our psyche pretty well.

HARRIET: *The School of Life sometimes ascribes secular "patron saints" to people struggling with various problems. Whom would you nominate as the patron saint of bad ideas?*

ALAIN: At a time when there are many bad ideas, it pays to remember the 19th-century German philosopher Hegel. In his *Lectures on the Philosophy of World History*, published in 1830, Hegel offers us a way of looking at the darker periods of history that neither glosses over their pain nor refuses to give up hope. Hegel saw a consistent pattern in history: He believed that the world makes progress by lurching from one extreme to another as it seeks to compensate for previous mistakes, and generally requires three moves before the right balance on any issue can be found. Hegel's argument can be a consolation at moments when it seems that one kind of progress has been entirely lost. He is on hand to reassure us that we are merely seeing the pendulum swing back for a time—that big overreactions are eminently compatible with events broadly moving forward in the right direction. The dark moments aren't the end; they are a challenging but necessary part of an antithesis that will—eventually—locate a wiser point of synthesis.

HARRIET: *When we've experienced a setback, how can we muster the confidence and energy to give it another shot?*

ALAIN: Often what holds us back from trying again is a fear of failure. To get over this, we need to make ourselves totally at home with failure, rather than attempt to evade it. Pessimism has a bad reputation, but it is one of the kindest and most generous of philosophies. That's because often what makes us sad and angry is the sense that our hopes have not come true

and that our lives are unusually bitter—that we have been singled out for particular punishment. Pessimistic ideas suggest otherwise. Life isn't incidentally miserable, they tell us; it is fundamentally difficult for everyone. This functions as an antidote to the oppressive modern demand to look on the bright side and allows us to bond with others around an honest admission of some truly sobering realities. Life can only ever be a process of replacing one anxiety with another. The greatest part of our suffering is brought about by our hopes—for health, happiness and success. Therefore, the kindest thing we can do for ourselves is to recognize that our grief is not incidental or passing but a fundamental aspect of existence.

HARRIET: *It's easy to say that forgiving yourself is the first step, but how do you actually do it?*

ALAIN: We need to try to become an imaginary friend to ourselves. This sounds odd, initially, because we naturally imagine a friend as someone else—not as a part of our own mind. But there is value in the concept because we know instinctively how to deploy strategies of wisdom and consolation with our friends that we stubbornly refuse to apply to ourselves. If a friend is in trouble, our first impulse is rarely to tell them that they are fundamentally a shithead and a failure. We try to reassure them that they are likable and that it's worth investigating what might be done. A good friend likes you pretty much as you are already. Any suggestion they make, or idea they have about how you could change, builds on a background of acceptance. They don't think there's anything wrong with giving you a compliment or emphasizing your strengths. It's quite galling how easily we can lose sight of all of our own good points when troubles strike. But the friend doesn't fall into this trap; they can acknowledge the difficulties while still holding on to a memory of your virtues. It is ironic—yet hopeful—that we know quite well how to be a better friend to near strangers than we know how to be to ourselves. The hopefulness lies in the fact that we do actually already possess the relevant skills of friendship. It's just we haven't as yet directed them to the person who probably needs them most—namely, of course, ourselves.

How To:
Ask for Help

From a young age, we are taught by parents, teachers and even fairy tales about the value of helping others. But very little is said about the flip side: the importance of asking for help when we need it. Particularly for those of us working without nine-to-five office hours and established workplace hierarchies, asking for assistance can feel like a minefield pitted with social faux pas and our own inhibitions. Harriet Fitch Little bit the bullet on behalf of all nervous help-seekers out there and sought the counsel of two people who've trained themselves, and many others, to get better at making the ask: executive coach Nora Bouchard and professor of clinical entrepreneurship Noam Wasserman.

HARRIET FITCH LITTLE: *Nora and Noam, the two of you have dedicated a lot of time over the last few decades to thinking about the idea of help and how we might get better at asking for it, but you've come to the issue from very different angles. Nora, am I right in saying that your engagement was sparked by a personal incident?*

NORA BOUCHARD: Yes. About 15 years ago I was going to have some surgery and found myself without anyone to care for me postoperatively. I realized that I had created this wonderful life with all the trappings of success, but I was surrounded by people who wanted to be helped, not necessarily people who were going to help me. I even broke up with my partner. It really drove a point home, and that's when I decided I needed to spend more time working on this topic. In 2007, I wrote my book, *Mayday! Asking for Help in Times of Need*, which was an amazing experience in itself simply because so many people were willing to help me with it. As a leadership and executive coach since the mid-'90s, I regularly see my clients resist asking for the help they need, and I know what they struggle with because I've been there too.

HARRIET: *Noam, you're coming to this from a more academic perspective. In your 2012 book,* The Founder's Dilemmas, *you amalgamated data from nearly 10,000 founders, using it to identify the pitfalls that new entrepreneurs face. Where did help enter into the equation?*

NOAM WASSERMAN: It's an underlying theme throughout many of the dilemmas that I see. I've found that at every step of the way there is some punctuating point where founders

WORDS:
HARRIET FITCH LITTLE

are grappling with whether they should "do it alone" or find someone else to help, and then they're dealing with questions of what kind of help they need. And I'm not just a data guy. There is a lot of nonquantitative research I'm tapping into in my work—deep case studies on founders and dynamics within the team. The same theme emerges there.

HARRIET: *We all find asking for help uncomfortable. Certainly, those of us working a nine-to-five job will have resisted going to bosses and colleagues for assistance at some point because we don't want to give them the impression we're bad at our job. What's unique about the challenges faced by entrepreneurs?*

NORA: Becoming an entrepreneur means going off on your own and is a declaration of independence. It's a way of saying that you've got an idea that you believe in so strongly that you're willing to step away from existing support systems that you may have completely taken for granted. That's everything from making sure your printer is working to idea generation to even just talking to someone throughout the day. Realistically, entrepreneurs need all sorts of help, but it's that belief that they can make it on their own that drives them.

NOAM: What makes entrepreneurs different is that they are always "selling": They have to sell themselves; they have to sell their venture to customers and often investors; they have to convey the idea that they've got it all nailed down. That discourages them from showing that they need help because they fear it portrays weakness instead. And you've got to remember that sometimes they're even "selling" to themselves, convincing themselves that there's a good reason why they gave up the paycheck, why they left that steady job.

HARRIET: *Noam, you make an important distinction in your book between entrepreneurs who are willing to seek help and those who resist it. You conclude that those who ask tend to be more financially successful. Could you explain why?*

NOAM: Founders who go solo are often doing it for reasons of control, but it's a dangerous route to go down. The data shows that generally, the most successful founders are the ones willing to include others, even if it means ceding some power. They understand that involving lots of other people, as long as they're picking the right people, will help them grow the value of their company. You probably don't have time to do everything—from creating a strategy to sweeping the floor—and even if you did have the time, you probably wouldn't be good at doing all those things. By offloading tasks to people who can do them better than you can, you're free to focus on your key parts and the quality of the work increases.

HARRIET: *Let's start with the fundamentals. If I wanted to ask you for help in a situation where there was clearly little chance of reciprocity, how should I go about it?*

NOAM: I have found a delightful thing with entrepreneurs: As a class, they are extremely supportive, especially when it comes to helping those who are a couple of steps behind them. But the thing that people do wrong when asking for help is not doing their homework. If someone comes to me and says, "I need help thinking about how to go international from a strategy perspective," that's totally outside of my area of expertise. That's a red flag because you're broadcasting to me that this is probably a group email that you've sent to lots of people. You've essentially communicated that you haven't tried to find the way that I could help you best, and so I'm less likely to go out of my way to try and assist you.

NORA: You certainly need to have clarity within yourself about what you're really asking for. I hear from a lot of coaches who are just starting out and are interested in learning about the way I work. Typically, I'm very open to that, but at the same time I often suspect—and sometimes this is confirmed—that they are not looking for help or wisdom, experience or advice, but really they're looking for leads. I think, generally, in asking for help, people should approach it as a conversation, not simply as a question. That's more inviting to the person who is agreeing to help because they feel as though they can contribute to the problem-solving. And by framing your request for help as a conversation, you may realize that the thing you were originally asking about isn't what you actually need.

NOAM: If you walk in with a notebook and a pen, that's one of the main things that tells me you're serious about getting help and acting on it. If I'm meeting with someone and we're covering lots of terrain and there are a bunch of things I've said that seem to be impacting the person but they're not writing them down, that's a big issue. It's very innocuous, but I think it shows whether they actually came for real help or not.

HARRIET: *What if I work up the courage to make the ask but get knocked back?*

NORA: It's rare for someone to say no. But if they do, don't just shut down and say, "Thanks anyway, I really appreciate it." You have to say, "Well, will there be other circumstances in which you might be willing or able to help?" Explore that rather than just taking no as a no. Most people who are asked for help will say yes. Sometimes the no that comes out is still an opening—you need to be aware of that.

NOAM: Sometimes the person has the desire to help but not the bandwidth to do so. It's just bad timing for them. That's especially true if you get no response from the person. If you've done your homework and you're sure that they can help you in some way, then maybe try again—very courteously and without becoming a pest—one more time before dropping it.

HARRIET: *Those are great tips for specific interactions, but what about more general strategies? What's your advice for people who want to try to make asking for help a regular part of the way they live and work?*

NOAM: To flip the coin somewhat, make sure that your giving help is productive for the person receiving help. Sometimes you have to restrain yourself from being the helper. I spoke to a woman recently, a pretty successful founder, who is trying to force herself to delegate after decades of being very involved in her business. She has now adopted what she calls the rule of three: In any meeting, she can only speak up three times. She essentially has forced herself to let others get involved and to take ownership of their tasks, rather than relying on her to lead them by the hand. It's not that she's never going to weigh in on things, but she's going to pick three high-leverage points where she's going to be doing it. That's the process she's using to force herself to do productive, developmental delegation to her people.

HARRIET: *Nora, that anecdote reminds me of a personal strategy you discuss in* Mayday.

NORA: Yes! When I first set out on this research, my coach set me the challenge of asking for help three times a day. It felt very unnatural at first, and I started with small steps: On one occasion I asked for driving instructions to get to a meeting even though I already knew how to get there. But gradually I started to realize the power of asking, and the emotional connection that you could forge with a complete stranger by doing so. It also makes others feel great about themselves whenever they have a chance to help. Ever since then I've made a point of really asking for help on a regular basis.

HARRIET: *So, put your money where your mouth is! When was the last time you asked for something?*

NORA: Yesterday. A colleague and I have been thinking about creating our own start-up. So I reached out for advice.

NOAM: I'm brand-new to this school [the University of Southern California], so things come up every day that lead me to ask for guidance.

HARRIET: *Let's move on to forward planning. If someone knows they're moving into a job where they won't have ready-made support networks, how can they prepare?*

NOAM: People often aren't aware of the help they need, so they can't ask for it. They're so driven to go and accomplish their goal that they're blind to the holes that are evident to everyone else. One planning strategy is to make sure you have a trusted outsider you can turn to—fresh eyes that are hopefully more educated than yours. Passion might be a founder's magic, but it can also become their downfall.

NORA: I also believe it's important to think about assembling your own personal group of advisors. Nowadays, it's a lot easier to do that than it used to be. When I went off on my own in the mid-'90s, that whole idea of being your own brand, creating a life for yourself, was quite new, and we didn't have the kinds of support services that are out there now. Today, where I live in Michigan, 85 percent of businesses are either family-owned or small

> "It takes a village to raise a successful company. The myth of entrepreneurs as individuals who have pulled themselves up by their own bootstraps is changing as more people realize that a good team is what makes a company strong."

start-ups. Many of these are ad hoc services to help with HR, marketing and tech advice. We didn't have that when I started.

HARRIET: *The place that most people will instinctively turn for support will be their partner or family. Is that a good thing?*

NOAM: It can be, but it comes at a price. There's certainly a whiplash effect that spouses must endure. Entrepreneurs will either come home saying, "Honey, we're conquering the world. This is going to be huge," or else it's, "Honey, I'm going to have to go and get another job because this is failing." There might be no in-between, and the spouse might have no idea which of those extremes will walk in the door that day. In addition, it's hard to ask your partner for help because you might have had to sell them on why they should support you in your enterprise when you were first setting out, rather than painting an accurate picture of the challenges. That makes it harder to go and ask for the help that's needed.

NORA: While Noam was speaking, I was thinking of a client of mine who has a small start-up. He was having difficulties and would come home panic-stricken knowing this was the only safe place for him to talk. And it was driving his wife crazy; she was terrified every time he came home. She would go through all the problems that he was dealing with because he didn't feel like there was anyone else that he could ask for help.

HARRIET: *What's the solution for making that a productive partnership?*

NORA: In that case, they worked out an agreement about how he was going to come home every day and that he needed to wait, inquire about her and the kids and decompress. Then they would talk about the issues of the day. And it helped her become more helpful, because she was able to protect herself from his energy, so to speak. It gave him time to decompress before he shared with her everything he was scared of.

NOAM: To me, the key is that you speak to your spouse in "educating" mode, not "selling" mode. They need to under-stand in advance that there will be potholes along the road, and a bunch of challenges that you're likely to face. Every day is not going to be you walking in and saying, "We're conquering the world!" Then, when you do hit a pothole, you're going to have a far better support system. It's going to be a question of, "How can we work through this together?'"

HARRIET: *We've framed this discussion around the basic presumption that we should all be asking for help more often. Is this really an important goal to set ourselves?*

NOAM: Absolutely. One founder I studied told me that being a CEO is the loneliest job. The metaphor he used was that the founder is at the center of an hourglass: You have the board of directors above you, at the top of the hourglass. You have the team that's below you at the bottom of it. But you are alone in the middle. Amid that loneliness, you desperately need to find a way to get the outsider's perspective we have been talking about—someone to help you with thinking things through and seeing the things you're missing.

NORA: Those who ask are the ones who get help. Most people are harder on themselves than they need to be. We all deserve to ask, and when we do, we reap amazing benefits: connection, an easier life and even new opportunities that could lead to greater success.

HARRIET: *And, finally, should there be limits to what we can ask for? The devil's advocate in me wonders whether those who choose to strike out on their own should be prepared to deal with the consequences.*

NORA: I think it's important to be able to tap into other people's wisdom and their experience. Now, if you're asking someone to come in on a monthly basis to do your books, brainstorm marketing or to help you do testing, I think that's a different relationship that you have to establish up front. With anyone that you ask for help, you need to listen carefully to make sure it doesn't become burdensome.

How To:
Adapt to Success

While it may seem counterintuitive, success can ruin a business. There are myriad ways in which problems can arise as a company grows, from day-to-day professional challenges to leaders finding themselves at the head of a growing team without any experience. Gloria Ware advises others on how to plan for and manage success at JumpStart Inc., a nonprofit organization helping diverse and ambitious entrepreneurs economically transform entire communities. She spoke with Charles Shafaieh about the challenges of working with investors, the threat of burnout and the importance of taking time to give back to others.

CHARLES SHAFAIEH: *How might entrepreneurs find themselves victims of their own success?*

GLORIA WARE: Initially, there's a lot of euphoria around raising capital without realizing what comes with it. Sometimes there's difficulty making that transition and understanding that once you have brought investors to the table, you need to listen to different opinions that you might not necessarily agree with. It's about adapting and building those relationships with your board and advisers. It's about doing things a little differently than you would as an individual founder and transitioning to thinking that this is *a* business rather than *your* business.

A lot of people will pursue entrepreneurship because they like the idea of independence, but investments bring additional responsibility. The investors are there because they have a keen interest in the company—you just happen to be its founder. They're investing heavily in the founder, but they're also looking at the founder's capabilities in terms of growing the company and generating a return on their investments. Therefore, it's very important to be discerning about who your investors are. It's almost like a marriage. You have to learn how to navigate the differences of opinion and to trust one another.

CHARLES: *Financial problems can ruin relationships, or so goes the warning.*

WORDS:
CHARLES SHAFAIEH

GLORIA: Absolutely, and raising capital is difficult! Entrepreneurs need to be discerning about whom they're choosing to receive capital from. Don't just look at it from a perspective of dollars but other assets too, such as expertise.

CHARLES: *Is there any way to prepare for these problems before you are confronted with them?*

GLORIA: Entrepreneurs should have an advisory board—a group of individuals they respect that are tactically chosen because they bring value. Get into a pattern of meeting on a quarterly basis. An investor wants to know that an entrepreneur has a team they can turn to for advice along with access to networks and other sources of capital. I don't know how much of that is teachable, but appreciating and valuing feedback from seasoned individuals who are either serving as mentors or as advisory board members, as opposed to formal board directors, is essential.

CHARLES: *Entrepreneurs should never isolate themselves then?*

GLORIA: It takes a village to raise a successful company. The myth of entrepreneurs as individuals who have pulled themselves up by their own bootstraps is changing as more people realize that a good team is what makes a company strong and that it's okay to ask people for advice. You need great counsel, great networks and expertise surrounding you to make good decisions and do more.

CHARLES: *When success arrives, the tempo of a company will inevitably change. You may need to innovate to satisfy your investors' needs, which may not be your own. How sustainable is the idea that you can stay successful under new pressures?*

GLORIA: Typically, in those first years, even if you've raised millions of dollars, the pace is very quick. You're constantly learning as you expand into different markets. There are always new competitors and things to learn. It's a constant chase, particularly if you're trying to set yourself up to be acquired.

CHARLES: *Regarding competition: In the beginning, you might not know who else is out there and what surprises might arise, such as other companies copying your designs.*

GLORIA: Entrepreneurs should know the competition and understand that the pace can change very rapidly. You should always be tapping into whatever is on your customers' minds and developing new products and services from that research. Typically, investors want to know what you're doing to make sure you're staying ahead of your competition—who you have on your team, what your approach is and how that's going to enable you to move quickly and stay ahead of the market. One of the things we strongly believe in is having people from diverse backgrounds and experiences on your team who bring insights that help you avoid groupthink. Then, how are you leveraging those unique skills to make sure that they are adding value to the company?

CHARLES: *When companies reach a certain size, power, as well as money, can have strange effects. How have you seen people react to these changes?*

GLORIA: I have seen people who've achieved success want to do something meaningful, like giving back to their communities or to other entrepreneurs. They understand the struggle and want to invest in the next generation of entrepreneurs.

CHARLES: *In other words, once you're successful, don't hide.*

GLORIA: You have to balance your image and your brand in terms of what people are expecting you to do as a business versus your actual capabilities and limitations. Even if you're

"One of the things we strongly believe is having people from diverse backgrounds and experiences on your team who bring insights that help you avoid groupthink. Then, how are you leveraging those unique skills to make sure that they are adding value to the company?"

very successful, there's always that next company that could potentially disrupt you, so you can never totally relax. All of a sudden, there's a lot of demand—to speak at events and conferences, for example, or to serve on boards. Entrepreneurs have to find a way to balance their time. Giving back can be a way of helping your co-workers and also managing your time to avoid burning out.

CHARLES: *Keeping your sanity must be difficult throughout this process. Is it important to maintain a healthy life outside of the business too? Mentoring would be one way to do that, but it's still company-focused in a way.*

GLORIA: I just read an article that argues that every entrepreneur should have a hobby. You're compelled to want to work 24 hours a day, but it's not good for you and eventually it catches up. Your body just says *stop*. I do find that happens to a lot of entrepreneurs at some point, and they realize that they have to take time out. I know one entrepreneur who schedules his workouts on his calendar! There's another myth, particularly for entrepreneurs who are newer to the game, that there's no time to have any other interests and that it's hard to pull away because there is a lot going on. It can make it really challenging for entrepreneurs who have families.

CHARLES: *Do you think that we have been conditioned to interpret success in a certain way?*

GLORIA: For some people, success is measured in the number of employees they have or in selling their company for hundreds of millions dollars. But I've had people tell me, "No, that's not what success looks like to me. Success looks like starting a business, being able to take care of my family, providing great customer service and value to the people

I'm serving." These people—some of whom are solo entrepreneurs but also those who have many employees—are not interested in raising venture capital because it means losing control of the business and the pace of growth they want to experience while also raising a family.

There are so many more options now in terms of choosing the type of business and how quickly you want to grow it. I ask people, "What is your big vision for the company?" Sometimes I encourage entrepreneurs to dream bigger. Sometimes that's not what they want. I have to determine if they're not aware of opportunities to scale or they're not thinking big enough, or if it's a matter of wanting to go slow and having this type of lifestyle. It's up to individuals who are advising entrepreneurs to be very intellectual about working with them on those things, understanding how a person sees their business development and growth.

CHARLES: *Decisions are going to entail risk. How does an entrepreneur cope with that uncertainty, both at the beginning and as success (hopefully) builds?*

GLORIA: Having a data-driven mind-set is important. We always look at things from a perspective of who your customer is, what problem you are solving for them and how big your solution is—is it a bandage or surgery? Ask what you're doing in terms of always having research and development internally so that you aren't caught off guard. Again, have a good team. It's why you have your board of directors—people who have had experience making these types of decisions and who are informed in the industry. Leverage that expertise, and also build relationships with other entrepreneurs who are going through the same thing or have been there before you.

How To:
Work Together

For better or worse, dynamics in the workplace can be a delicate ecosystem. To learn how to manage conflict and grow more attuned to one another, Molly Rose Kaufmann invited leadership coach Kari Uman and clinical psychologist Murray Nossel to advise on collaborating more constructively.

MOLLY ROSE KAUFMANN: *Please tell us about yourselves and how your work relates to group dynamics in the workplace.*

KARI UMAN: I'm a leadership coach, and I frequently work with women who are being promoted or who are starting a new job or position. Many women hold onto myths about how to be a leader—for instance, that working hard will automatically get you a promotion. Workplace values have radically changed in recent years, and I help individuals cope with these changes.

MURRAY NOSSEL: I'm a clinical psychologist with a PhD in social work and anthropology. In the '90s, I evolved a listening and storytelling methodology to teach people how to connect with one another. My company, Narativ, applies this methodology to a business setting. When I started Narativ in 2006, it was unheard of to share personal stories at work. People said to me, "Are you nuts?" But in 2017, the landscape has completely changed. People recognize that sharing and listening are important strategies for connecting and building trust within an organization.

MOLLY: *How do sharing and listening build trust?*

MURRAY: My method holds that there is a reciprocal relationship between listening and telling. Let's say that there is something going on in a team that everybody knows about, but no one is talking about—for instance, someone is going to be laid off. What are people on the team experiencing? Fear, paranoia. They might start feeling competitive with other people because they wonder who is going to be next. The lack of transparency breeds suspicion. What kinds of stories are going to be produced in that environment? Paranoid and fearful stories.

If you want to get people to communicate with one another in a way that is generative, creative and open, you have to teach them how to listen to one another without judgment. This is particularly difficult in a competitive environment because people are trying to survive and they feel like their

WORDS:
MOLLY ROSE KAUFMANN

survival depends on climbing on top, dominating or competing with someone else.

MOLLY: *Are there strategies that a leader can employ to encourage open communication?*

MURRAY: You can't expect intimate conversations to happen spontaneously in the course of day-to-day discourse. You have to create a dedicated time and space. You also have to give people very specific guidelines on how to listen and talk to one another. It comes more easily with a little bit of guidance.

KARI: Everybody rolls their eyes when you encourage them to share their personal experiences at work. "Why do we have to talk about feelings?" Well, the reason we talk about feelings is that when people feel they are being heard, they are more likely to develop trust.

One of the things that I train people to do is to actively listen. If a listener is really present, nothing else is going on in their head. They are not trying to come up with a witty response. They are paying attention to the content of the conversation. When you listen in this way, you paraphrase the content that somebody has told you, and you also clarify and help them acknowledge their feelings.

Active listening is about helping people get clear on their feelings and then move beyond them. I often tell people that they might as well talk about how they feel because their feelings are written all over them anyway.

MURRAY: Most people have difficulty expressing their feelings openly. It's scary to let the lid off personal storytelling—people are terrified that some Pandora's box will open and there will be a free-for-all of emotional expression.

MOLLY: *Kari, you mentioned outdated tropes in the workplace, that many people—women, particularly—feel that hard work is enough to get you promoted. Could you elaborate?*

KARI: Getting ahead within the workplace—within any group—is not just about hard work, or even good-quality work. Networking, getting out of one's office, taking risks, being proactive—these are the qualities that get you promoted. Success is predicated on building healthy relationships because ultimately people want to work with people they like. This goes doubly for women, who from an early age are often taught to be polite, soft-spoken and compliant, and to put

the health of the relationship above their individual needs. These behaviors run counter to those that actually move people ahead in the workforce.

MOLLY: *Do you observe differences between how each generation approaches these notions?*

KARI: Yes. I do a lot of work in the federal government, where you have boomers [ages 52–70] and millennials [ages 19–35] working together. Millennials are often better at being assertive in the workplace. Women from older generations were taught not to toot their own horns, but the younger generation has learned the value of standing up for themselves and taking credit for their accomplishments. I think that shows real progress.

MOLLY: *Does the changing economy influence how people relate to each other at work?*

MURRAY: The workplace is like any other communal setting, but it's bogged down with inherited conversations and antiquated narratives. One of the inherited conversations is this idea of efficiency. The industrial revolution produced a relationship to the manufacturing of goods in which the human body was equated with a machine. What you wanted to get out of the human body was maximum efficiency with minimum breakdown.

The problem is that we no longer live in a manufacturing economy. We live in an informational and service economy in which the human being—the being, the beingness of humanity—is now the vehicle. Our imaginations, our ability to innovate and our ability to solve problems are the requirements of today's workplace. We're not meant to simply function like machines. So we're applying these antiquated, obsolete messages from the industrial revolution to the way that companies work today. It's time to move on, and to recognize the collective intelligence that exists in a company.

MOLLY: *Is it possible to shift dynamics that seem entrenched?*

MURRAY: I'll answer with a story: In 2005, I went back to my hometown of Cape Town, South Africa. I was hired to do a workshop that ended up being totally packed with people. One man had come all the way from the Transkei—a 600-mile journey—because he was the storyteller in his village. Some women started to tell their stories, mostly to do

"Getting ahead in the workplace is not just about hard work, or even good-quality work. Success is predicated on building healthy relationships, because ultimately people want to work with people they like."

with family members dying of AIDS. Most of the women in the room were crying. I asked people to reflect on the stories that had been told and the man said, "This is the problem with women: They are weak. They cry at the drop of a hat." The women got angry and started to tell him off.

I asked the women to form a circle around the men, and for the men to form a group inside the circle of women. Then I asked the men to tell stories about what it is to be a man. The man who had offended the women told his own story. He had grown up in a very rural area and his father was a goatherd. He had looked after goats since he was five years old. He went out barefoot and stayed with the goats the whole day while the girls in his family went to school. So from that, he concluded that girls were weak because they couldn't be goatherds and went to school and needed shoes, while he went without shoes and school. As he told his story, the women's relationship to him changed. What had sounded like a sexist remark was totally altered. They were able to develop a tremendous empathy for the life he had lived.

And then, of course, I got the men to sit in a circle around the women and listen to their stories of what it meant to be a woman. You can create those kinds of atmospheres when people are willing to listen to one another through sharing their personal narratives. They come to a deeper understanding of one another that is not based on reaction or judgment.

MOLLY: *Do you think sharing personal stories and feelings helps teams to work together?*

KARI: When people open themselves up, they are sharing genuinely from the heart. And that's where the empathy comes in. It's heart-to-heart, instead of head-to-head. Once people connect to each other, they are less fearful of being in conflict. When people trust each other, only then can they truly engage in constructive conflict. High-performing teams need to be able to have conflict and discuss things. And if they cannot manage conflict at all, then a commitment to the mission or the objective flies out the window.

If you do not have the commitment, then who is accountable to whom? Ultimately, it all falls apart. Organizations end up with teams that have a great deal of conflict, a lot of stuff not being talked about. But usually, it *is* talked about in small groups—over a drink, in the bathroom, in pairs. Amazing conversations happen in the bathroom, instead of around the table where they should be happening.

MURRAY: How can we possibly imagine a world in which people are able to talk to one another across divides—ancient conflicts, sometimes—if we cannot even do it in our own relatively safe, relatively contained groups? I work with people to identify what gets in the way of their ability to listen to one another. If we come to our relationships with a whole bunch of assumptions, judgments and opinions that are already formulated, then we're never really open to finding out who other people really are. We're listening to everything through the lens of our own preexisting filters.

I'm training people to take a good look at what those filters are and to be ruthlessly honest about how they truly see things. What are the cognitive and emotional habits they use when viewing other people? When you can examine how you're listening to people, then people are much freer to tell their stories. In my training, teaching people how to listen to one another is always the prerequisite for teaching people how to open up to one another.

What is a corporation if it is not a community of people? And that community of people can choose how they are going to relate to one another. It starts with how teams relate to one another. This radiates to the rest of the corporation and then to the rest of the world.

How To:
Exert Caution

On an episode of *Donahue* from the mid-1970s, we see the host, Phil Donahue, welcoming Halston to the studio. "Is anyone a bigger hit in this business than you?" he asks the designer, leaning in with chummy reverence. "Is there anything left that doesn't have your name on it?" Halston, dressed as usual in a black turtleneck, smiles politely. He has the relaxed demeanor of someone accustomed to idolatry.

Watching this footage now, it's hard to imagine that the man being interviewed was once the lynchpin of America's fashion industry. Halston was the first celebrity designer, the first to open his own boutique, a pioneering figure in defining the aesthetic of minimalist elegance that came to characterize American design. He stamped his trademark on everything from carpets to underwear to Girl Scout uniforms. Donahue's praise was not sycophantic: In the 1970s, Roy Halston Frowick really was everywhere. But a decade later, quite suddenly, he would be nowhere and nobody. He was a shooting star of New York's halcyon disco days—a visionary entrepreneur who came crashing down to earth.

Halston was a man of modest Midwestern stock who arrived on the New York scene with a straightforward understanding of how he would transform fashion: "The simpler the better." According to Elaine Gross, who co-authored *Halston: An American Original* in 1999, it was a radical disruption to the fashion norms of the 1960s. "It was an era of more is better, when so many fashions were looking more like costumes than apparel that newly liberated women could comfortably wear," says Gross. "Halston's fashion philosophy was diametrically opposed."

Halston had begun his career as a high-society milliner (clients included First Lady Jackie Kennedy, for whom he designed the famous pillbox hat) and had learned a lot from talking to customers in the intimate setting of the hatmaker's salon. "Let's face it, dresses are not going to have feathers and fuss in the future," he told *Women's Wear Daily* as early as 1964. "We'll go on simplifying ... everything uncluttered."

In 1968, he made his vision a reality when he struck out on his own, swapping hats for dresses and setting up as Halston Ltd. in a showroom off Madison Avenue. His originality was instantly apparent. Halston cut fabric on the bias and endeavored to make dresses as close to seamless as possible. His looks were monotone: comfortable cashmere two-pieces, fluid chiffon caftans and simple shirtdresses. According to designer Ralph Rucci, a Halston protégé, the impact was in-

WORDS:
HARRIET FITCH LITTLE

stantaneous. As he put it in the 2011 documentary *Ultrasuede: In Search of Halston*, "Everything was obliterated. Nothing looked tasteful anymore."

It wasn't long before Halston needed a bigger canvas. In 1973, when he was bringing in just short of $30 million annually, he sold his company to the conglomerate Norton Simon Industries. The deal, worth $16 million at the time, made Halston an instant millionaire and "the envy of every designer on Seventh Avenue," according to *The New York Times*.

It was a calculated move. Halston was desperate to expand, particularly into fragrances, and Norton Simon owned Max Factor, so was well positioned to help. It was also, although only hindsight could know it, the moment that Halston sowed the seeds of his downfall: He had sold the rights to his own name.

For a long time, it didn't seem to matter. Halston's contract ensured that he maintained creative control over the label during his lifetime, and his personal stock had never been higher. "Will Halston take over the world?" was the headline that *Esquire* magazine chose for a 1975 profile of the designer. With Norton Simon behind him, it seemed possible. Halston expanded his headquarters into a stupendously expensive studio at the newly built Olympic Tower—a "glass box in the sky" in the words of one former model. Fresh orchids and perfumed Rigaud candles maintained an around-the-clock atmosphere of heady extravagance—appropriate given that Halston was by now spending his nights hosting hedonistic soirees at his house and at the infamous Studio 54. Bianca Jagger, Elizabeth Taylor, Lauren Bacall and Liza Minnelli were his friends and his clients. Andy Warhol was on hand as unofficial paparazzo at his parties.

He was also working extremely hard. Halston leveraged his move to Norton Simon to full effect, and expanded the label in directions that few high-end designers had dared to. As he boasted to *New York* magazine in 1974: "I've done the impossible feat for a designer, which is to have a store, made-to-order, retail, wholesale, movie stars, the works. And make a lot of money."

There was more than profit driving this rampant expansion. Halston was, according to those who knew him, a true patriot who dreamed of, one day, "dressing America": He designed the Team USA Olympic uniforms in 1976 and a new range of Girl Scout uniforms in 1978. He had ready—although it never came to fruition—a design for the New York Police

Department that included uniforms for pregnant officers. But it was Halston's vision of dressing an entire country that brought about his undoing. In the early 1980s, he signed a billion-dollar deal with the mass retailer J.C. Penney—a stratospheric amount of money for a collaboration, even by today's standards. The logic, as recalled by colleagues in *Ultrasuede*, was one of scale: "If your customers come to you in a limousine, you'll go home in a bus. If they come to you in a bus, you'll go home in a limousine."

But Halston hadn't reckoned with the fallout. Not only was his workload suddenly enormous, but he was also abandoned by high-end stockists who were embarrassed to be associated with a down-market store. Suzanne Hadler, chief marketing officer at Halston Heritage, points out that he had no role models for the collaboration. "Halston was doing this from scratch," she says. "Designers today have a lot more research and data about how to do these things well . . . We can point to a bunch of partnerships and say, 'Okay, that one worked, that one didn't.'"

A perfect storm was brewing. Halston was overworked, the J.C. Penney line was selling poorly, his image had taken a beating and his drug use was becoming far more than recreational. His fate was sealed when Norton Simon was sold, then sold again—a scenario that Halston had failed to anticipate. He was ultimately beholden to bosses at Playtex, or "bra and girdle men" as he disparagingly called them.

The designer was left stranded. Sidelined by new management who considered him an unwelcome liability, he was barred from using his name or even the monogram RHF when he tried to leave and establish himself from scratch. Until his death in 1990, he fought to regain control of his business. (Halston died of an AIDS-defining illness, and was one of the first celebrities to openly acknowledge that he was HIV positive.)

Not long before his death, Halston had sent a letter to his journalist friend Marylou Luther with ideas for the autobiography that they were planning to write. He already knew what he wanted the first line to be: "You're only as good as the people you dress," an observation that he had always been fond of making in interviews.

It must have been a painful maxim to remember at a point in time when he was dressing nobody. But, judged against his own standard, there was at least a time when Roy Halston Frowick was the best in the business.

Written by Leonard Koren, *Wabi-Sabi for Artists, Designers, Poets & Philosophers* offers insight into the Japanese art of finding beauty in imperfection.

Understanding a Photograph is John Berger's seminal collection of essays on photography—a call to look deeper than appearances.

Naoto Fukasawa and Jasper Morrison compiled *Super Normal: Sensations of the Ordinary* as an ode to all of the hard work, testing and failing that went into the tools and objects we use every day.

Supplies:
Read Up

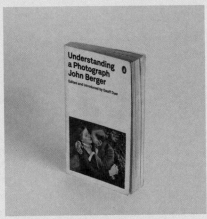

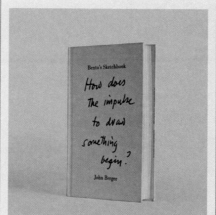

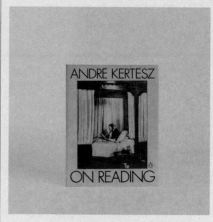

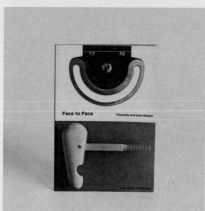

In *The Art of Creative Thinking*, Rod Judkins explores how we can transform ourselves, our businesses and society with a deeper understanding of creativity.

In *Face to Face*, François and Jean Robert offer a class in seeing things other people don't: in this case, everyday objects that resemble faces.

Bento's Sketchbook is John Berger's meditation on how we perceive and seek to explore our ever-changing relationship with the world around us.

The Pleasures and Sorrows of Work is philosopher Alain de Botton's exploration of the joys and perils of the modern workplace.

In *On Reading*, Hungarian photographer André Kertész explains how he gained inspiration for many of his best shots though his absorption in reading and the written word.

Every business has its reasons for existing in society: "No matter what you create, it's important to imagine yourself as a client," writes Japanese designer Kenya Hara in *Designing Design*.

A story a day: Miranda July's short stories in *No One Belongs Here More Than You* can each be read in a single sitting—preferably on a lunch break.

Brenda Cullerton's biography of Geoffrey Beene offers insight into and a deeper understanding of the fashion designer's illustrious and industrious career.

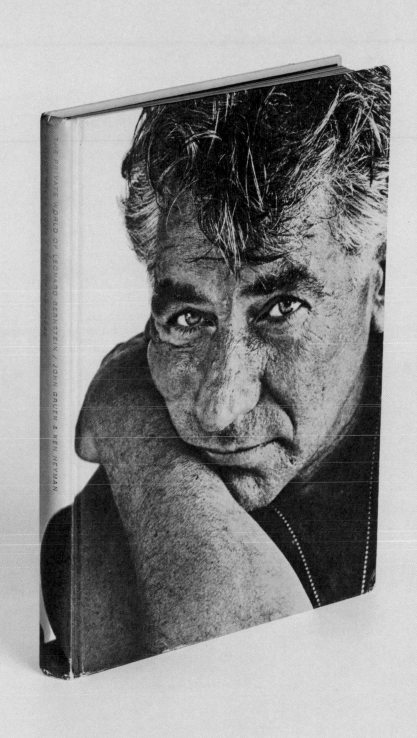

Vacation inspiration: *The Private World of Leonard Bernstein* features photographs of the composer's summer holiday in Ansedonia, a sun-washed Roman town on the Italian coast.

Supplies:
Desk Essentials

Is it lunchtime yet? Count down the minutes with a desk clock, like this LEFF Tube Clock designed by Piet Hein Eek.

Music can enhance productivity, improve moods and foster creativity. Tivoli's Model One BT radio is small enough to keep on any desktop.

Late nights at the office require cozy lighting. This JWDA Concrete Lamp from Menu features a dimmer switch.

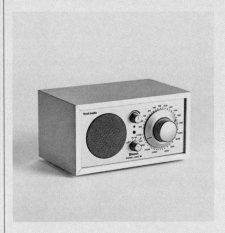

For anyone who eats at their desk: Keep keyboards crumb-free with a computer brush like this one from Asakusa Kanaya.

An old-fashioned paperweight, like this opalescent glass version from Canoe, makes messy piles of paper look intentional.

Neat environments can produce good habits: Use a desk tidy, like this design by Jonah Takagi.

Keep a candle on hand, like this Goober from Talbot & Yoon, to help scent office air and add to a calm, clean atmosphere.

Perhaps the most essential item is somewhere to record inspiration, like this heavy-duty, linen-bound notebook from Canoe.

Designed by GamFratesi for Skultuna, this Karui tray is an ideal catchall for small stationery, business cards and sundries.

Invest in timeless, durable basics. This solid
brass pencil sharpener has been in production
by German company DUX since the 1950s.

Look smart: This Print Prologue notebook features a thumb index for quick access to the important notes inside.

COVER	PRODUCTION	MACHINE
	Risograph	Riso RZ220
FLAT SIZE	FINISHED SIZE	STOCK
10.27 in. × 7 in.	5 in. × 7 in.	Astrobrights Lift-Off Lemon 80 lb. Cover
INK	FINISHING	BINDING
1/0, Black Ink, Exterior Only	Trim, Score, Fold	Perfect Bound
INTERIORS	PRODUCTION	PAGE COUNT
	Digital	48
INK	FINISHED SIZE	STOCK
1/1, Light Black, Kodak Dry Ink (Toner)	5 in. × 7 in.	Accent Opaque Digital White 60 lb. Text

Risographs ed. 1

Breathe some life into the workspace with a changing display of plants, foliage and seasonal flower arrangements.

The ballpoint pen was once considered an entrepreneurial idea. For designers, this German construction pen from Canoe features a built-in spirit level and ruler.

Coffee has fueled intellectual conversation since the Enlightenment period. Continue the tradition at your workspace with this cup by HAY.

Shrub, a refreshing drinking vinegar, has a long history in the Middle East. INNA Shrub produces a plum version that pairs well with gin on particularly difficult days.

Working late? Keep up the momentum with an espresso made in this La Cupola espresso maker by Alessi.

Supplies:
Snack Time

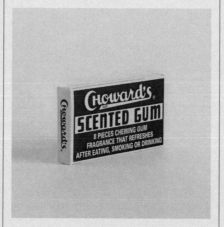

In 2014, professors from the University of Warwick in Coventry, UK, proved that employees who were given chocolate in the workplace demonstrated a 20 percent increase in productivity compared to those who were not. Pictured: Nathan Miller's Pretzel and Cherry chocolate.

In a 2013 survey conducted by online food ordering service Seamless, one-third of participants said that they would be more inclined to attend optional work meetings if complimentary snacks were provided. Pocky (pictured) is a firm favorite at *Kinfolk*.

Facilitate watercooler moments by placing a carafe and glassware in communal spaces. This glass is from Menu.

Keep energy bars like CalorieMate—a Japanese nutritional meal "block"—on hand when working against the clock.

It's thought that chewing gum may improve aspects of cognitive function and mood. Choward's Scented Gum has been getting the job done since the 1930s.

Accompany afternoon tea with mochi—
a traditional Japanese dumpling-like
sweet made from rice.

Entrepreneurial artist Lynn Read uses glass
left over from the creation of larger pieces to
create these tiny hand-molded glass salt bowls.

Tuna: The star of a thousand lunches-at-the-
desk. White tuna from Mediterranean producer
Ortiz is ideal for quick sandwiches and salads.

ドライ

ビール
STILLWATER
EXTRA DRY

Host a Scandinavian-style Friday bar for
co-workers and contacts. This Stillwater Saison
beer is brewed with rice and designed to
mimic the subtle flavors of sake.

The Last Word

Ten entrepreneurs offer one piece of advice
based on the skill set they needed to learn to
make their own businesses work.

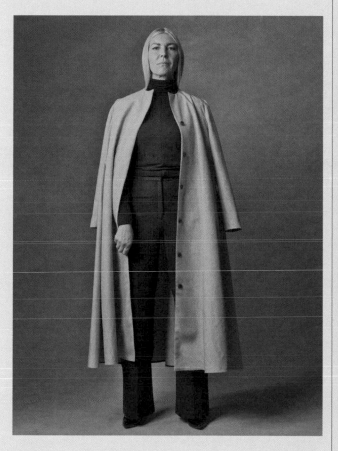

Hire a CEO

"Learn to pay for help with the things that you are not trained to do. It took quite a while before I realized that managing people and money is an actual professional skill. The best decision I ever made was to hire a CEO. It allowed me to concentrate on what I'm best at—the creative work. It was a matter of changing my attitude toward business: Earning money is necessary to facilitate your creative work. Finding the right CEO for the company has meant that I can concentrate fully on the creative part of the office and spend much more time on developing projects. The board, the CEO, my associated partners and I come up with financial strategies that make our work sharper and better."

Delegate

"I used to feel that it was somehow wrong to ask others to do things that I could do myself. It's taken me a long time to recognize that I need to concentrate on what I do best and delegate the rest. I think it hit me one day when I realized that I had almost no time for the creative work anymore. I started getting frustrated and feeling uninspired because I was spending most of my time on spreadsheets. There wasn't that uncontrolled space, where nothing was planned and inspiration could grow. Now that I have more space, creativity flows in a much more natural way. Some things are managed by my team, and I don't have to be a part of every little operation. I still feel in control, but only because I have also learned to let go."

Sell Yourself

"You can excel at what you do, but if you don't make yourself seen or heard, and if you don't know how to move in the world, then you aren't helping your business to work and grow. You have to know the right people, leverage your network and use word of mouth to gain more visibility. I realized that I had to change my business strategy and invest time in meeting more people—I had to take the leap to get out there and mingle. That's when I really understood the immense value in having a large network. I started to receive more acknowledgment on the design and art scene internationally, and that in turn helped with media interest. Mastering the art of public relations pushes me to keep on investing in my work, and motivates me to constantly move forward, create new design and never stand still."

The Art of Persuasion

"The art of persuasion is critical. An idea should work like a magnet that attracts talented individuals to it. I always listen carefully whenever I meet a client, but I make sure that I don't answer their request exactly—this would actually disappoint them. I started my design career in Japan, and I don't speak the language. Sometimes I didn't fully understand what the client was expecting of me, so I had to decide the potential of the project on my own. What you want and what the client wants will fuse together at a certain point, but it's so important to think ahead of what the client expects and keep the edge. If you present one concept that is exactly what was discussed, and another that is your own interpretation, the client knows you respected their vision but also knows you are ready to go beyond."

Build Bridges

"I often bring different partners together to work on projects that are not part of their core business. My skill here is empathy, and being able to understand what would incentivize and motivate each party. I need to be able to read what excites them and what turns them off, and collage together a cohesive vision. If you can't understand where someone else is coming from, then it's going to be a very difficult process. I used to only work with like-minded people—those who shared my unspoken language. But this is limiting. Seeing your ideas through other perspectives enriches them and gives them more dimension. So much inefficiency comes from failing to understand a situation from outside of your own narrow viewpoint. Empathy is fundamental to the success of any venture."

Reach Out

"Understanding consumers and consumer attention has been an extremely important skill to master. Social media helps me to create conversations with our customers, and then turn those conversations into transactions. You need to listen to your customers before executing anything. I realized that I needed to learn that skill once I started to reverse engineer brands that I wanted to emulate. Before, I thought that salesmanship and an independent spirit were the most important skills for an entrepreneur. I was wrong. I failed many times, but I failed forward. That was only because I acted on the feedback I received from our customer base. Social media and paid marketing have allowed us to reach 500,000 people on a weekly basis—something that would have been impossible for us years ago."

Know Your Craft

"Soon after starting Casa Dragones, I realized that in order to innovate and deliver something truly different in the tequila industry, I needed to become an expert in tequila making myself. So I learned about production, the harvest, the distillation process and many other technical aspects of the tequila business. As a result, I earned the title of Maestra Tequilera—the first woman in my field to receive this recognition. In fact, the Tequila Regulatory Council needed to change the title from Maestro Tequilero to the feminine, Maestra Tequilera, in order for me to receive the recognition. Having this level of expertise in a company allows one to innovate. For me, it's meant improving our production process to maximize sustainability, and to deliver sipping tequilas that are better than any others in taste and complexity."

Get Organized

"Let your people own their roles and career paths, and put systems in place to allow them to achieve their goals. You need to have the knowledge and experience to know that there are many paths to a desired outcome. Implementing well-articulated processes sets people up for success. The processes that we established in the early days, although they seemed like overkill at the time, were expandable and allowed us to scale up for our business today. They also allowed us to apply our energy and focus in other areas because we knew the job was getting done. The collective collaboration of people fighting for the same thing is far better than a single-handed approach to battling it out on your own."

Deal With It

"Very early on—as soon as I started working with people and getting busy—I learned the importance of management. I've learned how to manage a brand, a project, a business, work-life balance and working with a team, while also making sure everyone's got the space to bring their best to the table. I hit thousands of walls. And that's why these skills are so crucial: You need to know how to hit a wall and then negotiate your way over it, or better still, see it well in advance and have a ladder standing by. Because unless you can manage projects, situations, issues, challenges and opportunities all at once, it'll turn to chaos in seconds. The fashion business is all about imagination, ideas and pushing boundaries. In order for those elements to thrive, you have to have a very strong structure in place. Once you've got that, creativity can flow and come to fruition."

Pay Attention

"I've had to learn mindful communication, and how to avoid the temptation to go on autopilot. I had hit this kind of automation in the way that I was approaching my work, and I found that it took away the joy of problem-solving and made it difficult to see what was being asked of me. So I've learned to truly listen in the moment. Your brain only knows what it knows, and you have to actively engage it to zig when you know it's easier to zag. Constantly reminding myself that no two interactions are alike has been a necessary challenge. And it's turned out to be critical—now I can offer answers, expertise and communication from a far more aligned place. This has helped me add and derive value from even routine interactions."

Address Book

ANGELA OGUNTALA

INDUSTRY:
CREATIVE CONSULTANCY
FOUNDER:
ANGELA OGUNTALA
ESTABLISHED:
2013
LOCATION:
COPENHAGEN, DENMARK
WEBSITE:
ANGELAOGUNTALA.COM

APPARATUS

INDUSTRY:
LIGHTING DESIGN
FOUNDERS:
JEREMY ANDERSON &
GABRIEL HENDIFAR
ESTABLISHED:
2012
LOCATION:
NEW YORK, USA
WEBSITE:
APPARATUSSTUDIO.COM

ARMANDO CABRAL

INDUSTRY:
FOOTWEAR DESIGN
FOUNDER:
ARMANDO CABRAL
ESTABLISHED:
2008
LOCATION:
NEW YORK, USA
WEBSITE:
ARMANDO-CABRAL.COM

AZÉDE JEAN-PIERRE

INDUSTRY:
FASHION DESIGN
FOUNDER:
AZÉDE JEAN-PIERRE
ESTABLISHED:
2012
LOCATION:
NEW YORK, USA
WEBSITE:
AZEDEJEAN-PIERRE.COM

BROWNBOOK PUBLISHING

INDUSTRY:
PUBLISHING
FOUNDERS:
RASHID & AHMED BIN SHABIB
ESTABLISHED:
2006
LOCATION:
DUBAI, UAE
WEBSITE:
BROWNBOOK.TV

BYREDO

INDUSTRY:
PERFUMER
FOUNDER:
BEN GORHAM
ESTABLISHED:
2006
LOCATION:
STOCKHOLM, SWEDEN
WEBSITE:
BYREDO.EU

CASA DRAGONES

INDUSTRY:
FOOD AND BEVERAGE
FOUNDERS:
BERTHA GONZÁLEZ NIEVES,
ROBERT W. PITTMAN
ESTABLISHED:
2008
LOCATION:
NEW YORK, USA
WEBSITE:
CASADRAGONES.COM

COQUI COQUI

INDUSTRY:
HOSPITALITY
FOUNDERS:
FRANCESCA BONATO,
NICOLAS MALLEVILLE
ESTABLISHED:
2003
LOCATION:
YUCATÁN PENINSULA, MEXICO
WEBSITE:
COQUICOQUI.COM

CURIOSITY

INDUSTRY:
DESIGN
FOUNDER:
GWENAEL NICOLAS
ESTABLISHED:
1998
LOCATION:
TOKYO, JAPAN
WEBSITE:
CURIOSITY.JP

DAMIR DOMA

INDUSTRY:
FASHION DESIGN
FOUNDER:
DAMIR DOMA
ESTABLISHED:
2007
LOCATION:
MILAN, ITALY
WEBSITE:
DAMIRDOMA.COM

DESIGN ARMY

INDUSTRY:
GRAPHIC DESIGN
FOUNDERS:
JAKE & PUM LEFEBURE
ESTABLISHED:
2003
LOCATION:
WASHINGTON, DC, USA
WEBSITE:
DESIGNARMY.COM

DIMORE STUDIO

INDUSTRY:
INTERIOR DESIGN
FOUNDERS:
BRITT MORAN,
EMILIANO SALCI
ESTABLISHED:
2003
LOCATION:
MILAN, ITALY
WEBSITE:
DIMORESTUDIO.EU

DORTE MANDRUP ARKITEKTER

INDUSTRY:
ARCHITECTURE
FOUNDER:
DORTE MANDRUP
ESTABLISHED:
1999
LOCATION:
COPENHAGEN, DENMARK
WEBSITE:
DORTEMANDRUP.DK

FANTASTIC FRANK

INDUSTRY:
REAL ESTATE
FOUNDERS:
TOMAS BACKMAN, MATTIAS KARDELL,
SVEN WALLÉN
ESTABLISHED:
2010
LOCATION:
STOCKHOLM, SWEDEN
WEBSITE:
FANTASTICFRANK.SE

FRIDA ESCOBEDO

INDUSTRY:
ARCHITECTURE
FOUNDER:
FRIDA ESCOBEDO
ESTABLISHED:
2006
LOCATION:
MEXICO CITY, MEXICO
WEBSITE:
FRIDAESCOBEDO.NET

GALLERY YVES GASTOU

INDUSTRY:
ART
FOUNDER:
YVES GASTOU
ESTABLISHED:
1986
LOCATION:
PARIS, FRANCE
WEBSITE:
GALERIEYVESGASTOU.COM

GESTALTEN

INDUSTRY:
PUBLISHING
FOUNDER:
ROBERT KLANTEN
ESTABLISHED:
1997
LOCATION:
BERLIN, GERMANY
WEBSITE:
GESTALTEN.COM

HAY

INDUSTRY:
INTERIOR DESIGN
FOUNDERS:
METTE & ROLF HAY,
TROELS HOLCH POVLSEN
ESTABLISHED:
2002
LOCATION:
COPENHAGEN, DENMARK
WEBSITE:
HAY.DK

HENDER SCHEME

INDUSTRY:
FOOTWEAR DESIGN
FOUNDER:
RYO KASHIWAZAKI
ESTABLISHED:
2010
LOCATION:
TOKYO, JAPAN
WEBSITE:
HENDERSCHEME.COM

HERSCHEL SUPPLY CO.

INDUSTRY:
RETAIL
FOUNDERS:
JAMIE & LYNDON CORMACK
ESTABLISHED:
2009
LOCATION:
VANCOUVER, CANADA
WEBSITE:
HERSCHELSUPPLY.COM

HIKARI YOKOYAMA

INDUSTRY:
CREATIVE CONSULTANCY
FOUNDERS:
N/A
ESTABLISHED:
N/A
LOCATION:
LONDON, UK
WEBSITE:
N/A

HONEYCOMB PORTFOLIO

INDUSTRY:
INVESTMENT
FOUNDERS:
AZITA ARDAKANI,
MARISSA SACKLER
ESTABLISHED:
2016
LOCATION:
LOS ANGELES, USA
WEBSITE:
HONEYCOMBPORTFOLIO.COM

HYPEBEAST

INDUSTRY:
PUBLISHING
FOUNDER:
KEVIN MA
ESTABLISHED:
2005
LOCATION:
HONG KONG, CHINA
WEBSITE:
HYPEBEAST.COM

JOSEPH DIRAND ARCHITECTURE

INDUSTRY:
ARCHITECTURE
FOUNDER:
JOSEPH DIRAND
ESTABLISHED:
1999
LOCATION:
PARIS, FRANCE
WEBSITE:
JOSEPHDIRAND.COM

Address Book

KAREN CHEKERDJIAN

INDUSTRY:
FURNITURE DESIGN
FOUNDER:
KAREN CHEKERDJIAN
ESTABLISHED:
2001
LOCATION:
BEIRUT, LEBANON
WEBSITE:
KARENCHEKERDJIAN.COM

KAREN WALKER

INDUSTRY:
FASHION DESIGN
FOUNDER:
KAREN WALKER
ESTABLISHED:
1989
LOCATION:
WELLINGTON, NEW ZEALAND
WEBSITE:
KARENWALKER.COM

KOLLEKTED BY

INDUSTRY:
RETAIL
FOUNDERS:
ALESSANDRO D'ORAZIO,
JANNICKE KRÅKVIK
ESTABLISHED:
2004
LOCATION:
OSLO, NORWAY
WEBSITE:
KOLLEKTEDBY.NO

LIFE

INDUSTRY:
FOOD AND BEVERAGE
FOUNDER:
SHOICHIRO AIBA
ESTABLISHED:
2013
LOCATION:
TOKYO, JAPAN
WEBSITE:
S-LIFE.JP

MINÄ PERHONEN

INDUSTRY:
FASHION DESIGN
FOUNDER:
AKIRA MINAGAWA
ESTABLISHED:
1995
LOCATION:
TOKYO, JAPAN
WEBSITE:
MINA-PERHONEN.JP

MUBI

INDUSTRY:
FILM
FOUNDER:
EFE CAKAREL
ESTABLISHED:
2007
LOCATION:
LONDON, UK
WEBSITE:
MUBI.COM

NILUFAR

INDUSTRY:
FURNITURE GALLERY
FOUNDER:
NINA YASHAR
ESTABLISHED:
1979
LOCATION:
MILAN, ITALY
WEBSITE:
NILUFAR.COM

PIERMONT

INDUSTRY:
HOSPITALITY
FOUNDER:
RUPRECHT VON
HANIEL-NIETHAMMER
ESTABLISHED:
1992
LOCATION:
TASMANIA, AUSTRALIA
WEBSITE:
PIERMONT.COM.AU

POILÂNE

INDUSTRY:
FOOD AND BEVERAGE
FOUNDER:
LIONEL POILÂNE
ESTABLISHED:
1932
LOCATION:
PARIS, FRANCE
WEBSITE:
POILANE.COM

RONAN & ERWAN BOUROULLEC DESIGN

INDUSTRY:
DESIGN
FOUNDERS:
RONAN & ERWAN BOUROULLEC
ESTABLISHED:
1997
LOCATION:
PARIS, FRANCE
WEBSITE:
BOUROULLEC.COM

SEVEN UNIFORM

INDUSTRY:
FASHION DESIGN
FOUNDER:
TOKUJI MOTOJIMA
ESTABLISHED:
1952
LOCATION:
TOKYO, JAPAN
WEBSITE:
SEVEN-UNIFORM.CO.JP

SOPHIE HICKS ARCHITECTS

INDUSTRY:
ARCHITECTURE
FOUNDER:
SOPHIE HICKS
ESTABLISHED:
1990
LOCATION:
LONDON, UK
WEBSITE:
SOPHIEHICKS.COM

STUDIO NITZAN COHEN

INDUSTRY:
PRODUCT DESIGN
FOUNDER:
NITZAN COHEN
ESTABLISHED:
2007
LOCATION:
BOLZANO, ITALY
WEBSITE:
NITZAN-COHEN.COM

SWEET SABA

INDUSTRY:
CONFECTIONARY
FOUNDER:
MAAYAN ZILBERMAN
ESTABLISHED:
2015
LOCATION:
NEW YORK, USA
WEBSITE:
SWEETSABA.COM

THE PROPER SNEAKER

INDUSTRY:
FOOTWEAR DESIGN
FOUNDERS:
SONIA TANOH,
CAMILLE TANOH
ESTABLISHED:
2014
LOCATION:
NEW YORK, USA
WEBSITE:
THEPROPERSNEAKER.COM

WANT LES ESSENTIELS

INDUSTRY:
ACCESSORIES DESIGN
FOUNDERS:
BYRON & DEXTER PEART
ESTABLISHED:
2006
LOCATION:
MONTREAL, CANADA
WEBSITE:
WANTLESESSENTIELS.COM

WOOYOUNGMI

INDUSTRY:
FASHION DESIGN
FOUNDER:
WOO YOUNGMI
ESTABLISHED:
2002
LOCATION:
PARIS, FRANCE
WEBSITE:
WOOYOUNGMI.COM

YVONNE KONÉ

INDUSTRY:
FASHION DESIGN
FOUNDER:
YVONNE KONÉ
ESTABLISHED:
2011
LOCATION:
COPENHAGEN, DENMARK
WEBSITE:
YVONNEKONE.COM

Thank-Yous

First, we would like to thank the people featured in this book for making the time to welcome us into their workspaces and for so readily sharing their hard-earned business acumen. Thank you for your patience and generosity and for the work that you do that inspired us to create this book in the first place. The same thanks extend to those people who were kind enough to invite us into their offices but are not featured.

A wholehearted thanks to the photographers and writers around the world that so beautifully captured the stories featured in this publication. It is an honor to work with such talent and we feel privileged to be able to publish your work.

Thanks to the *Kinfolk Entrepreneur* team: Anja Charbonneau, John Clifford Burns, Amy Woodroffe, Molly Mandell, Rachel Holzman and Tracy Taylor for the hard work, creativity and endurance it took to bring this book to life. Thanks also to our colleagues at *Kinfolk*: Doug Bischoff, Julie Cirelli, Nikolaj Hansson, Mario Depicolzuane, Monique Schröder, Frédéric Mähl, Jessica Gray, Paige Bischoff and Hanna Ruahala for their invaluable insights, ideas and immutability.

Thanks to Alex Hunting for envisioning and executing the design of this publication down to its very last detail, and to the wonderful assistants who supported the project at various stages: Ulrika Lukševica, Lucy Ballantyne, Daniel Norman, Lucrezia Biasutti, Margriet Kalsbeek, Charlotte Long and Federico Sher. Thanks also to stylist Sidra Forman.

Thanks to model Mbaye Ndiaye—the man on the cover of this book—and to cover photographer Paul Jung, casting director Sarah Bunter and stylist Jessica Willis, plus Allie Smith and Lizzie Arneson at BRIDGE for hair and makeup. A special thank you to our assistants Benja Pavlin and Océane Torti for creating the artwork featured on the back cover.

Thanks to Mako Ayabe, Kota Engaku, Akaya Okamura and all at Kinfolk Japan for your advice, assistance and tenacity in producing and translating our stories in Tokyo. Thanks also to Takahiro Goto, Yoshiko Takahashi and Mariko Takahashi.

Thanks to our publisher, Lia Ronnen at Artisan for your ideas, feedback and support throughout the project. Thanks also to Artisan team members Bridget Monroe Itkin, Zach Greenwald, Sibylle Kazeroid, Michelle Ishay-Cohen, Renata Di Biase, Nancy Murray, Hanh Le, Allison McGeehon and Theresa Collier.

Thanks to Canoe in Portland, Oregon, Spring Place in New York, Les Deux Magots in Paris, Nordic Bakery in London and The Lab in Copenhagen. We would also like to extend a special thanks to Samuel Åberg at Moon Management, Geneviève Brière-Godfrain at Poilâne, Drew Schufman at Supervision, Tania Sutherland at MUBI, John Shegda and Brooke McClelland at See Management, Mikey Evans at Starworks Group and Martina Gamboni.

And lastly, we would like to thank our readers. Without your continued support, we would not be able to do the work that we love to do. Thank you.

Credits

Library of Congress Cataloging-in-Publication Data

Names: Williams, Nathan, 1986- author.
Title: The Kinfolk entrepreneur / Nathan Williams.
Description: New York City : Artisan, a division of Workman Publishing
    Co., Inc. [2017]
Identifiers: LCCN 2017018001 | ISBN 9781579657581 (hardcover : alk.
    paper)
Subjects: LCSH: Businesspeople—Biography. | Entrepreneurship. |
    Cultural industries—Biography.
Classification: LCC HB615 .W552 2017 | DDC 338/.040922—dc23 LC
    record available at https://lccn.loc.gov/2017018001

33614080451437

Design by Alex Hunting

Artisan books are available at special discounts when purchased in
bulk for premiums and sales promotions as well as for fund-raising or
educational use. Special editions or book excerpts also can be created to
specification. For details, contact the Special Sales Director at the address
below, or send an e-mail to specialmarkets@workman.com.

Published by Artisan
A division of Workman Publishing Company, Inc.
225 Varick Street
New York, NY 10014-4381
artisanbooks.com

Artisan is a registered trademark of Workman Publishing Co., Inc.

Published simultaneously in Canada by Thomas Allen & Son, Limited

Printed in China

First printing, September 2017

10 9 8 7 6 5 4 3 2 1